The King Inside You

Third Edition

Written by
Enock Ofori

Copyright 2022

PUBLISHERS

The King Inside You
Third Edition
© Enock Ofori

ISBN: 978-81-949457-1-0

3rd Edition Published in 2022 by
Mage Orange Publishers
An imprint of Mage Orange Publication & Technologies
1st Floor, Reena Apartment, Kamakhya Nagar,
Adabari Tinali, Guwahati-781 012, Assam (India)
Phone : +91 7086-521-682,
Email : info@mageorange.com | info.mageorange@gmail.com
www.mageorange.org

This Book was forwarded by;

RT. REV. DR. EBENEZER K. ABAKA-WILSON.

DIOCESAN BISHOP; METHODIST CHURCH GHANA, CAPE COAST.

Third Edition

*This book is based on the original manuscript
by the writer without any editing.*

- The Publisher

Dedication

This book is dedicated to YOU, the reader. Your silence, love, care, motivation, support, and inspiration as a mentor, father, mother, brother, sister, and friend have been beneficial to me. Words cannot elucidate how grateful I am as a brother and a friend to you than honouring you with this book. For that, I thank you.

Acknowledgment

This book is a testimonial manifestation of the glory of the Highest God. I am again deeply grateful for the inspiration, motivation, and wisdom of people who, through their lives, encouragement, instructions, directions, corrections, and commitment, have contributed to the success of this book. For the advancement and production of this book, I am with much gratitude to acknowledge these reputable personalities for their immeasurable contributions to the success of this book:

MR. YEBOAH EMMANUEL, MRS. ASIEDUAA MARGRETT, AND MR. ADU STEPHEN.

Table of Contents

Introduction

You may experience a series of emotions as a result of reading this book: apprehension and relief. Unless we know our purpose in life, we are often unaware of how important we are to the world. This false belief that we are unimportant and have no connection to the world or the people around us is one that we often succumb to. In the grand scheme of things, what you become as a person is far more important than what you accomplish in the world. People's rejection will kill you if you live for their approval in your daily life. Because we're living in fear, we're not pursuing our dreams. When something happens for a reason, the hardest part is waiting for it to happen. And the better you is the reason for this.

God gives you a position where you can influence others and change the world. Sadly, we often miss the original intent of God's purpose and plans for our lives when we choose to pursue our interests and happiness. True, each of us is born with a specific purpose in accordance with our appointed monarchy and priesthood, which we can discover or completely miss. Who or what drives you to discover and maximise the potentials within yourself (THE SELF YOU)?

In pursuing life purpose, Everyone must ask themselves these two outstanding questions everyone: the first question being, "Where am I going?" And the second one is "Who will go with me?" if you ever get these questions in the wrong order, then you must redefine the purpose of your life. You are here to bring a difference, to improve the world or worsen it. To either maximise your untapped potentials inside you or live purposelessly and die fullness with all your untapped potentials. And whether or not you carefully choose to, you will accomplish either one. My advice is, if you feel like you don't belong to this world, it's simply because you are here to assist in creating a new one.

Robert Brault has said an amazing statement: *"We are kept from our goal not by obstacles but by a clear path to a lesser goal."* You cannot go from absolutely nothing to something, so there must have always been something. You will meet the everyday challenges with a greater sense of life purpose as you align yourself with God and His assigned purpose for your life. You will begin to realise that God doesn't begin from the beginning but from the end. This book will guide you to realise and maximise your untapped potential in your life fulfilment. Therefore, this book is a blessing for every reader as you access the divine alignment of God to influence your life's purpose on earth.

1
DRIVEN TO DISCOVER
LIFE PURPOSE

Purpose by Influence

BECAUSE WITHOUT knowing our purpose in life, we are often unable to appreciate our significance. When we believe that our lives don't matter and have no impact on the world around us, we succumb to the illusion. *The Bible provides a wealth of information about what it means to be a human being and what it means to spend a meaningful life.*

> *"for we are God's handiwork, created in Christ Jesus to do good works, which God prepared in advance for us to do."*
> *Ephesians 2:10*

> *"But you are a chosen people, a royal priesthood, a holy nation, God's special possession, that you may declare the praise of him who called you out of darkness into his wonderful light."*
> *1 Peter 2:9*

The type of person you become in life is more important than your successes and failures in the world. Has this question occurred to you, "What is my life's purpose?" many people across all human races go through life feeling discouraged about themselves and thinking they don't have a purpose in life.

Whoever you are—whatever your life experiences, role, ability, talents, giftings or potentials, you have a purpose. You are not created empty; neither are you created as an accident. Our purpose and how we live them lead to fulfilment in life. In 1 Peter 2:9, two main keys are learnt: a **kingship** and a **priesthood**. To elaborate more on these two keywords, we must first ask how kings and priests influence their domains or territories? But how do we discover our life's purpose without first discovering our better selves as kings and priests in God's intended purpose for our lives? I have found out that in life, pursuing purpose, the process of discovering who I am begins with knowing who I don't want to be. Who then is a king and a priest, and how do we effectively influence our dominion scope with these privileges? I discovered these eleven (11) privileges that enthrone our kingship and priesthood in Christ through His aligned purpose for our original intent life purpose.

- A king cannot be voted out of his power: he was the king before his world began, and he will still be the king after it has passed away.
- A king's word is a law: no one can countermand his orders, negate his pronouncements, set aside his decrees, or amend statutes. His words are final.
- A king himself owns everything in his domain: a kingdom is the only type of government where the ruler owns everything and everyone. He has the power to dictate, and everyone adheres to his decree.
- A king's decree is unchanging.

- A king chooses a citizen: the people do not vote for the king, but in fact, he chooses them.
- A king embodies the administration of his kingdom: He is the king of Heaven because he lives in the hearts and lives of his people.
- His authority and power execute a king's presence: when the king shows up, his authority comes with him. Kingdom citizens may always exercise kingly authority as the king is always present with them.
- His property measures a king's wealth: the king of heaven owns everything, everywhere, in the realm of natural as well as the supernatural.
- A king's prosperity is gauged by the status of his citizens in his domain or territory. A citizen of the kingdom of heaven essentially prospers because the king of heaven is the wealthiest of all.
- A king's name is the testament of his authority: Jesus, the king, has delegated his authority to his citizens. He promised to do everything they asked in his name, and at the mentioning of Jesus name, all knees must bow, in heaven, and on earth and beneath the earth and must confess the Jesus Christ in the Lord.
- A king's citizenry represents his glory: The kingdom's citizens are to reflect the character of their king, who is just, righteous, compassionate, benevolent, and full of glory.

Isaiah the prophet said, "It is only what carries dominion that speaks to this generation." The great commission is not all about men being saved, that's one side of the victory, but being counselled out by the laws of the darkness that governs over a territory. The privilege for you as a king and a priest in your spheres of influence and dominion refers to any and every scriptural method deployed to enthrone Christ and his purposes to the heart of men and across every stratus in human activities. God is not interested in the unique method but in the motivation and the power that sponsors it. If that can happen through church service, then church service has now become a medium of advancing God's kingdom; if that can happen through giving birth, then giving birth has now become a ministry and a means of advancing His kingdom. If that can happen through singing, then singing is advancing His kingdom. If that can happen through business, then through the business, God's kingdom is advancing. We may look back and see a path we have taken through life someday to come. It will indeed be tempting to think that the path has always been there, laid out with purpose and waiting for us to walk on it. In Christ, we who are many forms one body, and each member belongs to all the others, just as all of us has one body with numerous members, and all of these members do not have the same role. According to our grace, we have different gifts, talents, potentials, visions, goals, and dreams. If a man's gift is prophesying, he should be able to use it in proportion to his faith.

> *"If it is serving, let him serve; if it is teaching,*
> *let him teach; if it is encouraging, let him*
> *encourage; if it is contributing to the needs of*
> *others, let him give generously; if it is leadership,*

let him govern diligently; if it is showing mercy,
let him do it cheerfully."
Romans 12:4-8

To each and everyone according to this strength and capabilities, God entrusted to him gifting.

I believe that immortal is not those who never die; immortal is those who don't hesitate to die for a purpose. The body's most important function is that all parts play a specific role to make it complete. It hardly matters which part of the body you are or your role; you have a purpose and a share in it. The key is, don't minimise your role. On the contrary, the seemingly weaker parts of the body are indispensable, and those we think are less honourable are those we treat with special honour. *"And the parts that are unrepresentative are treated with special modesty, and the body has given more honour to the parts that lack it."* Sometimes we can be so busy with our lives that we forget the purpose-designed for us. We are driven by the demands and necessities of life and do not realise that God always has a greater purpose for us. The purpose of our lives encompasses us and the lives of those around us as we join part of the body. In a more content way; **Submission to the direction of your Maker protect your life and the lives of others.**

In the Book of Genesis, Pharaoh mistakenly thought that he was in control of the people of God—the people of Israel. However, God placed him as an Egyptian leader for Him to achieve His designated purpose for His people. *For the Scripture says,*

"For this very purpose I have raised you (Pharaoh) up, that I might show my power in you, and that my name might be proclaimed in all the earth."

At times, your closers friends will rebel against you. At times, your loved ones will be the first to betray you when you need them most, but could it be that for God's will and His purpose in your life to be perfected, such betrayal must come? The betrayal of Christ was the purpose for mankind's salvation, the betrayal of Joseph by his brothers was for the purpose of saving his family from famine, the betrayal of John to exiled on the island of Patmos was to have an encounter with Christ to write about the deep things of God about the end time in the Book of Revelation. How will you describe these events? Are they coincident or God preordination's to establish His purpose? **God positions you to influence others and also to change evens.** But the tragedy is that we often miss the intent of His plans for our lives and decide to fulfil our personal interests and pursue life satisfaction. The preceding sentence truthfully states that each of us is born with a purpose in accordance with our ordained kingship and priesthood. We can either discover or completely miss that. The purpose of our lives has to always be at the forefront of our minds. We may be offered greater and more lucrative opportunities in life that may not fit in the realms of our primary ordained purpose. This requires wisdom on our part to wait on Him before making presumptuous decisions that may have lifetime ramifications. Hard times can make it seem difficult to see or witness the purpose of God, especially when we only feel pain and grief, and sorrow in our lives—like that of Jabez and Miphiboseth.

Many times, we don't wish to be reminded that He is working difficulty for our good. We are stormed by doubts and fears that often keep us from living out the purposes that He has established for us. Probably, a fear of aging catching up with us, a fear of not getting educated, a fear of relationship and marriage problems, a fear of failing in life, a fear of missing an opportunity by refusing to compromise our integrity, a fear of Chronic diseases, a fear of death. But the hard reality is that "To become the all, you must experience the all."

Unfortunately, so many of us go through life trying to figure out what we are supposed to do and missing every aspect of our purpose because they are so concerned about getting it right from scratch. In pursuing life purpose, everyone must ask themselves these two outstanding questions: the first one has to deal with, "Where am I moving?" And the second is "Who will accompany me?" if you ever get these questions in the wrong order, then you have to redefine your life purpose. You are here to bring a difference, Either to improve the world or to worsen it. And irrespective of whether you consciously choose to, you will achieve one or the other. My advice is, if you perceive that you don't fit this world, then perhaps you are here to help create a new one. He has a purpose for everyone, including those who resist Him.

Purpose by Dominion

IT MATTERS not only about what you know but the sequence of knowing. There is a sequence to the knowledge of the truth. There is something you should know about God before He blesses; if your prosperity becomes known to you before knowing that about Him, you become guilty, which will destroy you. So, there is a sequence and a foundation to the knowledge of God. There is a way God want to be known, and this is built according to a pattern. The acknowledgement that He is the source and the Sustainer of all things does something to Him. Consistently, in the realms of the supernatural, there is contention as to who is the Lord. The earth is the Lord thereof. In order of priority, the kingdom of the Lord comes first, which means the jurisdiction and the influence of a king. The presence of the influence of a government within a territory is what continuous to invent several needs. That means your needs are fulfilled when this influence finds expressions in your life. So, the problem is not lack of job, is not lack of good governance, is not lack of opportunities, the problem is not about witchcraft, the problem is not about geographical location, is not about wickedness, but that there is the absence of the influence of the government of God represented in a territory that has not yet experienced these realities. **Don't downgrade your dream just to fit your reality. Upgrade your conviction to match**

your destined purpose. According to His predetermine counsel, that's the intention of His purpose to find expression in your life. The will of God should be done not on earth but on earth. This portion of the earth represents you and your scope of influence that will reflect His kingdom. Not just about the physical territory.

The portion of the earth that will allow His influence to find expression in Him is His kingdom finding expression on earth through you (in the earth). To desire his influence, the dimension of His dominion, and His purpose finding expression in you. Many territories are around, but one has allowed His testament to finding expression of His will on earth. The extent of His power, governance, dominion, and purpose all must find expression in you. In the design of this earth, the man was the object of God's intended purpose to reflect His kingdom on earth. If you can find the expression of His kingdom in your life, it can only be extended to other territories. And any other approach that is not in this sequence will continue to frustrate our life purpose while we live on earth. The degree to which God's will and purpose come is the degree to which His kingdom manifests. The dealings of His power, glory, grace, dominion and influence of a man is a reveal and a manifestation of how much His will has found an expression in that man's heart.

The will of God is fulfilled in the realms of the mind. The system by which people receive the will of God is through transformation. "So, God prepares some vessels for honourable use and others for dishonourable use. For those who seek after God and try to follow Jesus, God will help them to be honourable vessels. Therefore, **if anyone cleanses themselves from what is dishonourable**, he will become **a vessel for honourable use**, set apart as holy, useful to the house leader, ready for all good work.

> *"This is a system by which you can embrace the*
> *will of God."*
> *Romans 12:2*

And still not be conformed to this world; but be transformed by the renewing of your mind, that yet prove what that good is, and acceptable, and perfect, will of God." A genuine transformation starts with transforming our mindset to receive the kingdom. Meaning after being transformed by the renewal of your mind, the potential of His will must reflect in your spheres of influence. This is more than a system of changing patterns and styles; it is a system of origination and complete transfiguration. To be subjected to His influence and ordinances. Our possibilities are a reflection of His transformation in our lives. A small mind limits the multifaceted potentials that are residence in Christ. A mindset is a sustained thinking pattern; it is a perspective and a viewpoint to control systems.

> *"Permit this mind to be in you which was also in*
> *Christ...."*
> *Philippians 2:5*

The sequential pedigree of your alignment with God is proof of the level of your mind transformation. **Lao Tzu once said, "Knowing others is wisdom; knowing yourself is Enlightenment."**

Some indices are attestations to our mind transformation. By the degree of your spiritual enlightenment, by the attestation of your influence, by measuring the fivefold kingdom prosperities: financial, mental, health, relationship, and spiritual prosperities. Your future and your life purpose are defined by the excellence of the transformation of your mind. Just because you are looking for it doesn't mean you will see; there is grace and alignment in this kingdom. We don't see with our eyes in this domain realm; we see with our mind, for the eyes just give a reflection of whatever your mind has seen. …Hagia couldn't see the water on the desert, …God was at Betel, but Jacob couldn't see, …there was a lamb for the sacrifice, but Abraham couldn't see. Could it be that since your mind has refused to see the employer inside you, your eyes only reflect you as an employee? Probably, it looks like you are left up alone in the wilderness, it looks like all hopes are lost, it looks like there is nothing better again because of the pain, sorrow and frustration you are going through. It seems your story is that of Ichabod: all the glory has departed, but could it be that you are not seeing the will of God and His purpose in your life. Who told you there is only one door? Can you not see that there are many open doors, for in a man's house are not only articles but articles and all are for purpose in that house? There is a door that leads to wealth, there is a door that leads to restoration, there is a door that leads to prosperity, there is a door that leads to influence, there is a door that leads to speed and divine destiny helpers, there is a door that leads to increase, there is a door that leads to honour, but all these doors are seen. Your mind must-see and your eyes must reflect them. The realms of this kingdom are a compendium of infinite possibilities and are only limited by the King's power who owns the kingdom. These possibilities are limited by the sight and the light we have. Your life purpose is your story; write well and edit often, for the church's glory is its dominion and influence over creation (territories).

2
THE UNTAPPED POTENTIALS

Fulfilling Untapped Potentials

POTENTIAL IS the kind of word that can bring joy, hope, and celebration. However, on the contrary, it can also bring about disappointment, dread, despair, failure,e and frustration. Unfulfilled potential is lamented as a waste and a mockery—he had so much going for him, but ...; her future was so bright, but ..., he started very well in life, but... On the other hand, fulfilled potential brings satisfaction and influence. I knew there was a certain speciality about that boy...; he was brought up very well..., God's mighty hands were upon him right from birth, and he has grown to be so influential..., he is a blessing to his family, this society and our nation at large... From the moment we enter into the world till we take our last breath, we are all judged by our potential and how we imparted our generation and the unborn generations.

Irrespective of our status, height or tone, the way we are perceived, received, accepted, or denied is based on what we can bring, offer or provide to the lives of our own and of those around us. Potential is seen differently depending upon the eyes we are looking through. What has great potential, according to you, may not look so great to me. You may be satisfied with going to basic school or high school, but someone else may aim for a doctorate or attain professor honour. You may be content with being a worker, but someone else desires to manage and lead an organisation or a company. You may be satisfied with a two-bedroom or a self-contain, but someone will be aiming at building an empire or an estate. God addresses you as

> *"a chosen generation, a royal priesthood, a holy nation, a peculiar people."*

God has nothing else but good thoughts for you. He was willing to offer His best so that He might regain the relationship that our sin took away from Him. In spite of what others may perceive, *God says,*

> *"I know the thoughts that I think toward you, said the Lord, thoughts of peace, and not of evil, to give you an expected end."*

In life, I have discovered that what God thinks about you and His plans for you should be what you should pattern your life after. I'm talking about **fulfilling untapped potential inside you**! The very essence of your life.

Peter and Isaiah find themselves in the presence of God and are each overcome with a sense of their sinfulness and inability. Isaiah cries out, "Woes is me for I am undone, for I am a man of the impure tongue, and my eyes have seen the Lord!" Peter falls at Jesus' feet, "Go away from me, Lord, for I am a sinful man!" This happens every time people find themselves in the presence of the blazing beauty, holiness and perfection of God. You can be good at something, but there is nothing like being in the presence of someone who is truly world-class to make you feel like a hack. Getting near to God is traumatic like that, but an order of magnitude more. All your many flaws are highlighted in the light of true Perfection, revealing all the hidden sinful secrets in you, and forcing you to see what's wrong with you. That is because we base much of our worthiness on our performance, our grades, our resume, being correct, good, hardworking, loyal, competent make us worthy. *"Everyone has inside of him a piece of good news. The good news is that you don't know how great you can be! How much you can love! What you can accomplish! And what your potential is!"* Whenever God peeps inside of us, He doesn't see the failures of the past—but rather the potential for our future. He sees potential in us; we have never seen or didn't even know we have. Let me ask each of us these two outstanding questions. Do we think that God can create astonishing opportunities even though they didn't previously exist? Do we think He has unlimited potential? One more question to do, do we believe the Word of God? **It's time for us to seize previously unknown opportunities and tap into those unused potentials.**

In the Book of Genesis, Joseph was someone who fulfilled his potential. Even though Joseph dreamed about God's greatness for him, several stumbling blocks could have prevented Joseph from becoming unfulfilled potential. He struggled through the following obstacles to arrive at his expected end: Friends and relatives sometimes kill our dreams and potentials in life. People sometimes can't see what God has a purpose for us. Dream Killers (His family tried to kill his dreams). Fractured support system (Family abandoned him). The Pits (He fell and still got up)? Integrity Thieves

(Potiphar's wife). Forgetful friends (Butler & Baker). Joseph was determined to fulfil his purpose despite all his obstacles because He knew what God had shown him, and he trusted God's plans for his life. He didn't wait to see it with his naked eyes before believing. He trusted God anyway. Can we do the same? Can we trust God even when it doesn't look like what He has said about us will come to pass? Is there anything too hard for Him? Allow Him to fulfil the potential He sees in you!

Overcoming the Poor Self-Image

THE WORD states that "children are an inheritance from the Lord," and we believe that every child of all ages has great potential. We dream for them to become doctors, lawyers, engineering, and a benefit to society. Even when they don't listen or meet your expectations, we still expect great things from them, and that is the level of faith we have as humanists. But the potential is not enough unless it is fulfilled. Our children at school perform based on potential. Adults, too, are judged based on their potential. Advancements in our jobs are also based on potential. If the company thinks that you can be or will become an asset to the company or the organisation, advancement opportunities will be made available to you.

For many years in my life, I saw myself as an average person, but when I got into the Word of God, He began to bring out abilities, giftings, goals, and attitudes in me, which helped me maximise my potential. 'The Book of Judges' is also a 'Book of Exploration' of the great potentials of leadership by people who had grieved fears when God called them to lead His people in times of persecution and afflictions by their enemies. They saw themselves as unqualified and poor self-image for the befitting portfolio of leadership. In this case, Gideon can be a common illustration who never noticed His potential until an angel revealed to him that he was a mighty man of valour. God saw potential in Gideon, but he didn't even know such potential existed in himself as he saw himself as a poor self-image.

> *"Gideon said to him, "Me, my master? How and*
> *with what could I ever save Israel? Look at me.*
> *My clan's the weakest in Manasseh, and I'm the*
> *runt of the litter."*
> *(Judges 6:15)*

After 40 years behind the desert, when God instructed Moses that he would be the deliverer of his people: the people of Israel, he questioned his potential integrity as unqualified and unprepared for leadership and all the opportunities of his past that had gone wasted. **Be spiritually and mentally prepared to open your hearts to accept what God is sending in your way.** The secret is that your previously untapped potential is for Kingdom effectiveness and advance. Do you want God to show you how to use previously untapped potential? Praise Him prior for the revelation and instructions he has for you. Fear kept Gideon and Moses from unleashing their full potential. It was fear of the unknown for Gideon and fear of past failures for Moses. You can find two leaders who doubted their abilities through a little fear of failure. People are held back due to their fear of failure, which prevents them from achieving their full potential. Joel Osteen said: **"I want to challenge you today to get out of your comfort zone. You have so much incredible potential on the inside. God has put gifts and talents in you that you probably don't know anything about."**

The Realms of Inside Out Discovery

MANY PEOPLE never unleash their full potential in life. Amidst our daily routines, it can be easy to fall back into old habits rather than try something new. It's still true that we all have a God-given inclination to live our lives to the fullest. It's enough for some people to sum up their entire lives in this way. However, deep down, we all know there must be more to life than this."

In essence, Jesus is saying, "Yes, there is!" There is a limitless amount of potential in every human being. In Jesus' eyes, you should strive to be a highly effective member of society. He wants you to produce 'a fruit—a hundred, sixty or thirty times what was sown.' The minimum is a thirty-times multiplication. Recognising who you are in God is what it takes to reach your full potential, not having ambition or success as a driving force. Those who seek God and live their lives in accordance with His plans will reap a bountiful harvest. Your influence grows as you begin to fulfil your God-given potential. He desires for you to have a prosperous life. Israel stood to gain tremendously from this opportunity. God wanted Israel to be a blessing to other nations, but he also wanted them to be a blessing to themselves. Your life can be even more blessed than those you've read about, both in the Old Testament and in the books of the Bible. *Jesus says,*

"Blessed are your eyes because they see, and your ears because they hear. For I tell you the truth, many prophets and righteous people longed to see what you see but did not see it, and to hear what you hear but did not hear it."

There will be a time in your life when you will be forced to either live within the potential of your faith or with the consequences of your doubt. The author of "The Greatest Salesman in The World," Og Mandino, once said: **"I am here for a purpose, and that purpose is to grow into a mountain, not to shrink to a grain of sand. Henceforth will I apply all my efforts to become the highest mountain of all, and I will strain my potential until it cries for mercy." Some people don't think they are creative or, sadly, don't have any potential for greater success.** If you believe this, it will limit what God wants to do in you and through your life. I challenge you to recognise, cultivate and manifest your previously untapped potential in your life. They are within you, and I challenge you to look down deep inside and tap those great but hidden potential inside to manifest outside (the Inside Out).

The Bible's story of the talents is a familiar one. One servant received five talents, another two, and the other with one. The Bible says, two of the servants used, or invested, their talents and increased them. The third servant hid him closely for fear of losing it. Those servants who maximised and increased their talents were given more, and the servant who fearfully adhered to his had it taken away and given to the servant with ten talents. As many times as you have heard this story from the Bible, how did you apply it to your own life? Perhaps you felt the story referred to people who had some special gift or talent, such as writing or acting, dancing, creating, designing or singing. Yet, when Jesus told this parable, He was not speaking to a multitude of imaginatively talented people or the past generations. He was speaking to skilled and unskilled workers—ordinary people like you and me—who He knew had extraordinary potentialities within them. Albert Einstein once said: **"The mind that opens to a new idea never returns to its original size."** How are you using your imagination?

Imagination is called the "scissors of the mind" because just as you use a pair of scissors on a bolt of material and that material becomes the reflected form that your scissors cut it into, so does your imagination work on the unspecialised substance of God all around you, and that substance becomes to you just the reflected form that your imagination gives it! Therefore, invest your talent of imagination wisely. See yourself well and strong if presently you are having a health challenge. See yourself making successful sales if you are in business. See yourself poised and confident in some situation that you may be dreading to face. The time must come—and let it be today when regardless of the facts, you choose to believe that you are an adequate person, a remarkable person, a successful person, a poised and confident person, because you know that you are a child of God. You choose to believe the teaching of Jesus that God is within you.

Follow the Principles

GOD has given us countless spiritual principles in the Bible. **These principles are fundamental truths, laws**, rules, and safeguard foundations for fulfilling our purpose in life. **On the other hand, it may be for specific circumstances**. His principles are practical, beneficial, and life-transforming for those who choose to know them and apply them in their life's fulfilment. Knowing about God's principle is like knowing where a piano is. Learning to apply those principles in life is like being able to play the piano. And just like playing the piano, being able to apply biblical principles also takes practice.

> *"I have hidden Your Word in my heart, that*
> *subject of discussion might not sin against You."*
> *(Psalm 119:11)*

David is saying that knowing the Word of God kept him from sinning. It shall do the same for us, too. I have discovered these five (5) principles for this book to guide you in tapping into previously unused potential.

Principle of Promoting Humility

HUMILITY IS a truthful approach to the reality of our lives, and it acknowledges that we are not more important than other people. On the contrary, "Self-importance is, therefore, the absence of humility." In the Book of Psalm, the psalmist says in his distress that it is the 'wicked' who seek to make themselves distant— 'and he rejects the laws of God'. They think of themselves as more significant than others—especially the poor, whom they 'draw into their net and crush'. These verses educate us about the pitfall of not being humble. When things go well in our life, it is tempting to say, 'Nothing will ever shake me and more dreadful to say that no one will ever do me harm. We can be tempted to think that we do not need God: 'In his pride, the wicked man fails to seek him; in all his thoughts, there is no room for God'. It's easy to become arrogant and boastful. One of the most prioritised prayers we ought to pray every moment is to ask the Lord to safeguard us and keep us from pride, arrogance, and self-importance. "May I seek you with all my will and heart, remembering that I need you and that you never forget me." This type of prayer is not a prayer of spiritual maturity only, but to ask God that you need more of Him and to know more of Him.

Principle of Pursuing Intimacy

THE BIBLE teaches that becoming a Christian means severing all relations with your family. In the Old Testament, the fifth commandment is 'honour your father and your mother,' but In the New Testament, *we are instructed that,*

> *"Anyone who does not provide for relatives,*
> *and especially for immediate family members,*
> *has denied the faith and is worse than an*
> *unbeliever,"*
> *1 Timothy 5:8*

Yet Jesus here indicates that something is more important than even your relationship with your family. That is your intimate relationship with Jesus and doing 'the will of the Father'. *Jesus says,*

> *"Whoever does the will of my Father in heaven*
> *is my brother and sister and mother."*

His words speak of intimacy, pre-eminence, prominence, and acceptance—a relationship at the deepest possible level. You can have this enriching closeness to Jesus. Stay near to him each day, and you shall fulfil your potential.

Principle of Purifying Yourself

J OYCE MEYER, who often speaks of the child abuse she suffered, writes: *"Have you, like Dinah, ever been an innocent victim? I can assure you that even in the worst circumstances, God gives us the grace to forgive so that we can go on with our lives."* In the Book of Genesis, one terrible crime (the rape of Dinah, Genesis 34:2) led to another. The retribution was not proportionate. God's people attacked the unsuspecting city, killed every male. They carried away all their women and children. The result was catastrophic. Jacob says, "You have brought grave trouble on me by making me unpleasant to the people living in this land. We are few, and if they join forces against me and attack me, I and my household will be destroyed." The actions of Simeon and Levi are profoundly condemned for their violence and their evil conduct of cruelty. In those days, to say the least, revenge was not just a pitfall for Simeon and Levi; once again, it was just a temptation for each of us.

When I am offended, I want revenge. In the Old Testament, retribution was limited by proportionality— 'life for life, eye for an eye, bite for bite, tooth for a tooth' and so on. Jesus sets (supported by his death and resurrection) an even higher standard for your relationships today. Forgive and be affectionate to your enemies. Jacob said to his household,

"Get rid of the foreign gods you have with you and purify yourselves." The promise to Abraham was that "A nation and a community of nations will come from you," so as you are also a royal priesthood, a holy nation, and a chosen generation. The potential is great. The influence is high, the vision is bright, but if we want to have a powerful impact for Christ to be enthroned in the world, we need to be people of purity as Rick Warren says, **'In ministry, private purity is the source of public power.'**

Principle of Putting Down Roots

SPIRITUAL HIGHS are important, but solid spiritual foundations must accompany them, or else there is a risk of shallowness and eventual disillusionment. Keep an eye out for this hazard. Even when we are doing the right thing, our hearts can fail us. Those parts of your life that no one else sees are where your spiritual roots are found. Praying, giving, and thinking are all part of this. When Jesus tells one of his parables, he refers to the seed that falls on shallow ground. Because it lacks a root, it grows quickly but quickly dies. The person who lacks roots can only last for a short time because of the difficulties they face. He explains later, "Make sure your spiritual roots are strong and healthy if you intend to reach your full potential."

Principle of Protecting Your Heart

I T IS CONVENIENT for people to get distracted by life's vicissitudes. Many things can fill your life and occupy your time for God and other ways to develop your spiritual roots. *The Scripture says,*

> *"Keep your heart with all vigilance, for from it flow the springs of life. Put away from you crooked speech, and put devious talk far from you. Let your eyes look directly forward, and your gaze be straight before you. Ponder the path of your feet; then all your ways will be sure."*

Solomon here refers to the things of the human heart, which the Bible uses to highlight a person's core, where their thoughts, feelings, desires, and choices begin. *The Bible teaches us that,*

> *"Out of the abundance of the heart, the mouth speaks,"*

which connotes that the heart is the seed of all deeds. This helps us understand that our thoughts often dictate who we become because the mind of a man or a woman reflects who they genuinely are. This is precisely why the Lord examines their heart. Because He knows their depths and sees into the inner motivations of the heart. The heart here is seen as the pivotal edge where all issues of life emerge from it. David pleaded with the people not to harden their hearts in rebellion against the Lord as they did in the wilderness. Getting the right view of the word of God and submitting in obedience to the teaching of Scriptures in all of our life endeavours is the best way to maximise our previously untapped potential.

3
PEN ISN'T MIGHTIER THAN SWORD

Your Future is Foretold

I HAVE LEARNT in life that whatever you are born to do is already done by God. He always begins with the ends before He starts. That means when God begins something, it is proof that He has ended it. Your future is His past. You are at the beginning of your end now. Futurologists are people who make predictions. A prediction says that some babies born now could live till the ripe old age of 150. Some consult futurologists to know what is coming. Others go further. Many people read their character descriptions and what will happen to them because they want to know what the future holds but sadly forget that outside of God's presence is nothing but total emptiness. *Jeremiah warns the people of God; the Israelites,*

> *"Don't for a minute listen to spiritualists and fortune-tellers, who claim to know the future."*
> *Jeremiah 27:9*

The time of Jeremiah is gone, and his words are bouncing back to us in the same way he warned his people. Only God truly knows the future, as he is the one who holds the past, present, and future in his hands, much of it is concealed from us. However, God tells you certain things about your future. We ought to ask ourselves, "Can the Pen be mightier than the sword?" Pens don't win battles, and swords don't write poetry. Mighty is the hand that knows when to pick the pen and when to pick the sword. You are an instrument of God. Don't ever think you are more and never believe you are less. Let God play beautiful melodies through you.

This perceptiveness contains one of the most wonderful and often quoted promises of God about His plans for our lives. Jeremiah was a true prophet. He heard the word of the Lord. However, there were some false prophets like Hananiah around. Jeremiah says, "The prophet who prophesies peace will be recognised as one truly sent by the Lord, only if his prediction comes true." Unfortunately, Hananiah's was one of the prophets by then whose predictions did not come true because the Lord had not sent him. Jeremiah's prophecies did come true. The people of God did go into exile just as he had warned. Now, Jeremiah speaks the message from the Lord to his people in exile. He tells them, *"Seek the peace and prosperity of the city to which I have carried you into exile. Pray to the Lord for it because if it prospers, you too will prosper."* There is a notable principle here. Generally, you should seek peace and prosperity for the place which God has ordained to you. This includes places you may work, your local church, your city and nation, and everything surrounding you. There is an expression: *"Bloom where you are planted."* This nudges you to stay put even if you're isolated or uncomfortable (like in exile). Even if you don't want to be where you are, it must be a good place for God's work to flourish in you if God has brought you there.

After seventy years in Babylon, God promises to bring his people home: *"I will come to you and fulfil my gracious promise to bring you back to this place,"* he says. The wonderful promises are framed in this way: *"My plans for you are to help and not harm you, and to give you a future of hope and happiness."* And I will hear your prayers when you call on my name. When you pursue me with all your heart, you will find me. "You will find me," I promise. God has good plans for you. They are not the plans for your failure or defeat. They are plans to 'prosper you'. They are not average or mediocre plans. They are good, pleasing, and perfect plans for your prosperity.

History tells us that studying our past helps us predict the future, so we need to understand the past to understand the future. We all face temptations, difficulties, sin, fear, sorrows, hope,s and desires. The psalmist says, 'I recounted my ways, and you answered me. He spreads his case before the Lord, opening his heart with sincerity to him. There are the times of deep sorrow: 'My soul is weary with sorrow' How does the psalmist respond to all his difficulties? He indulges in prayers, 'Preserve my life according to your word.' He meditates on God's word and prays: "Strengthen me according to your word. Keep me from deceitful ways; be gracious to me through your law." Resolve to follow God's ways in everything, but not out of any obligation or guilt. Choose to run in the path of His commands, for He has set your heart free. The psalmist does not conceal his feelings. He speaks about them openly and vulnerably: 'I am feeling terrible!'

So often, our 'struggles' rather than our 'successes' make us stronger. The Thessalonians' faith and love were growing despite—maybe even because of—the persecution and trials that they were enduring. Regarding their *short-term future,*

Paul writes, "We constantly pray for you, that our God may count you worthy of His calling, and that by His power He may fulfil every good purpose of yours and every act prompted by your faith." We are not simply sitting around waiting for Jesus to return as some of the Thessalonians seemed to have been doing. God has got a 'good purpose' for your life. He has called you. He is the one who fills your heart with ideas. He works inside you both to will and to act according to his 'good purpose.'

4
YOUR "FUTURE SELF"

Your Future is Not Ahead of You

THE FUTURE is not ahead of you; Instead, it is trapped within you. In my teenage years, I used to think the worst thing in life was ending up alone, but I have discovered that the worst thing in life is ending up with people who make you feel alone. I have learnt that it is very easy to raise when we are content to be exceptional in life. This demonstrates that You can build self-confidence by achieving goals that are far beyond your current abilities. As a result, it's time to begin envisioning a brighter future. This person, you think you need to let go of your grip on them. The idea that your future self will be a carbon copy of your present self must be abandoned. It's a lie, end of the storey.

Irrespective of how hard you try or how good your intentions are, your future self will be different. Inevitably, things will be different in the future. You can choose to grow or not. I believe that imagination is more important than knowledge. In other words, how much imagination are you willing to put into your own life? This dilemma can be solved by ignoring what others think of you and how they try to make you feel. People will look at you as a decent human being if you let them. There is nothing you can do to stop them from seeing you as a bad person. The more you try to present them with your good intentions, the more likely they will reject you as they are already convinced that you are a liar. The only way you can truly change yourself is to believe in yourself and not rely on others to do it for you. We are the designers of our reality! You don't have a future in front of you. Your future is hidden deep within you, just waiting to be unlocked, realised, and revealed. In many ways' society considers us out-of-date, and we sometimes buy into that as our reality. When we live in the darkness of not believing in ourselves, there is a space in our minds that we don't, very often, allow to be considered. That light, those images of ourselves living free of fear and disbelief in ourselves, that's our future. It's frightening, for sure. It seems like the same distance away as far as Pluto.

But, it's right here. It's with us every second of every day. The cool thing about our future is that we create it! It's not perfect because nothing is. It's not stress-free because that's not reality. Right, this minute, you are choosing to allow the new You to live in your mind. You are beginning to allow your future to manifest in bright living colour, inside your mind, where you can see and feel what it will be like. Keep creating that future; continue adding more detail. Let it grow. When I began excavating the future in my mind, I knew telling some friends (especially those my age!) about it would only result in undermining comments. So, I kept it hidden. It was my very own treasure. I knew that the life I had created in my mind would eventually be my Reality and my Testimony. There is a lot of exploration, a lot of freedom, so much fun ahead of you. Enjoy it in your mind—add detail and specifics. Eventually, add a timeline. Even if the date changes (which mine did on several occasions), you will Know: It's Time one day. Create it in your mind now. Create it in Reality, and don't refuse yourself a request you did not make."

Becoming "the Self You"

IF YOU PERCEIVE your present and future selves as two different people, then your likelihood of making better decisions today will improve. According to studies, most people are imperfectly predicting who they will be in the future. The reason is simple: it's much easier to remember the past than to visualise the future because we don't take the time to think of the future; we assume that things will more or less be the same in ten years as they are now. We even innocently believe we will be the same person in ten years as we are right now. We recognise that we have gone through some big changes in our past, and we mostly consider our current selves as the finished and evolved version of ourselves and conclude that we will mostly be who we are now in the future. If you ponder on who you were ten years ago, you will likely observe some differences. You were probably in a different situation. You probably had different goals, visions, potentials, and aspirations. You likely had a different environment, friends and hobbies. Of course, part of what you were doing is probably still the same. As people are aging, they tend to change less over 1-2 decades year periods of time.

From age 10 to 20, you're going to see some big change.

From age 20 to 30, you're going to see some big change.

From 30 to 40, you're likely to see some big changes as well.

But from 40 to 50, the rapidity of change tends to slow down for most people.

People often become less welcoming to new experiences as they age. They cease seeking novelty and change. They stop thinking of a bigger future. Their past becomes increasingly responsible in predicting who they are and will be. Their life becomes increasingly habitual. Your routine needs to challenge you beyond what you have ever done before continuously. The only way to be confident is by pursuing what you have never done before in life.

The Fivefold Strategies

The fivefold strategies for imagining and creating your desired future:

1. Imagine Who You Want to Become In the next decade
2. Imagine What It Would Feel Like to Be That Person Truly
3. Shift as Much as you can in Your Current Life to Reflect Your Future.
4. Expect Everything and Attach to Nothing
5. Measure the Gain, Not the Pain

Strategy One: Imagine who You want to be in the Next Decade.

It's difficult to get there if you don't know where or who you want to be. Your vision is your greatest asset." When you look at your future self as a distinct individual from the one you are now, you can begin to imagine what they might want. You need to have an eye for detail. What do you long to accomplish in the future? Are you able to see things in great detail? You won't have a chance to look forward to your life if you don't have a vision. To achieve a fulfilled life, you must have a goal to work towards, something to look forward to. Your new vision guides the way you look at your entire life as soon as you create it. It becomes the backdrop for everything you do. Changing the setting alters the perception of significance and potential.

So, let's get clear on your vision. You should not focus on how you are going to achieve the vision. You simply want to get very clear on what you want your next decade (10 years) to become from now. So, take out your calendar and mark a big X ten years in the future. How does your life look? How do you look like? What is the state of your surroundings? Who are the most necessary individuals in your life and on your team? What kinds of clients or individuals do you work with? What is your overall impression of the situation? What does a normal day look like for you? How much are you earning? What is important to you? What is your goal? Remember, it is not your task to determine how any of this stuff will happen right now. Your first task is simply to gain a clear vision. The clearer your vision is, the more obvious and easier will be the execution.

Strategy Two: Imagine What It Would Feel Like to Be That Person Truly

Once we are immersed in that scene, changes occur in our brains. Therefore, each time we do this, we are laying down new neurological tracks (in the present moment) that change our brain to look like the brain of our purpose and future. In other words, the brain starts to make an image as if the future we want to create has already happened." Once you have committed to something, your job is to shift your brain, mindset, and identity to match that future reality. Through

Visualization, creativity, action-oriented and focus, you call your future into the present (THE NOW), the new you. You want to see yourself reaching where you ideally want to be. This is an important distinction of life. All goals are not desired outcomes but desired versions of yourself. If you want a new future and a new you, you need a new version of yourself.

Strategy Three: Shift as much in Your Current Life to Reflect Your Future Self

Just visualisation isn't enough. You need to keep identifying evidence throughout your life that you are seriously chasing it. One of the most energetic ways to demonstrate the reality of your dreams is to begin investing in the future self that you envision for yourself. To prioritise your life effectively, you must first make powerful decisions in your own life. Who you allow in and out is entirely up to you. You have the power to define what success means to you. Resetting your expectations can be done by stopping to play other people's games. How much of your current life, environment, and behaviour match your desired future?

Strategy Four: Expect Everything, Attach to Nothing

One of the most common predictabilities is to lower your expectations so you don't get hurt. A question that has consumed my thought for many years, why are we so afraid of getting hurt? Your expectations play a huge role in your motivations and the results you acquire. I have discovered two prerequisites to being motivated: **You have to have some knowledge or competency as to how to get it, and you have**

to believe you can do whatever is involved in achieving that goal.

You increase your confidence by teaming up with other capable people. Your confidence increases with confidence. Often, people procrastinate because they don't know what to do and fail to make progress. They have an aim but have little skill or knowledge to achieve it. Thus, it becomes a dream unfulfilled and such a life tragedy. Your sphere of influence and sphere of dominion will begin to expand when you take action toward your dream, invest in that dream, and build a team around you. As a result of this progress, you'll feel more confident in your ability to. But the hard truth is, everyone must just choose one of these two pains: the pain of discipline or regret. It's your choice if you succeed or fail. Being bold and committed, and motivated is up to you. Of course, you are going to face painful moments. If the future you are pursuing is boldly bigger and different from your present, you will fall flat on your face a lot. It will be complex and confusing. You can and should get used to that. It just takes repeated exposure, increasing knowledge, commitment, and support. A flower doesn't compete with a neighbouring flower. It just blooms. Don't be discouraged. You are almost there.

What God is giving you require preparation, focus, commitment and patience. Discouragement is the enemy's favourite tool to use against you. He knows there is greatness within you. Keep your head up and high, and be confident in what you do. Be confident in your intentions and keep your eyes ahead instead of wasting your time on those who want to drag you back. A lot of self-help writers these days argue you shouldn't have goals because they make you feel horrible. You feel bad if you fail and are disappointed when you succeed, but never forget that you are bound to perish without purpose. The problem isn't in the goals or expectations. The problem lies in emotional attachment to the outcomes you will experience along the way. If you get used to pain and failure, nothing can stop you.

Strategy Five: **Measure the Gain, Not the Pain**

"The way to measure your progress is backward against where you started, not against your ideal." So, how then can you measure the gain while experiencing the pain?

Here is how it may work: Every season or year, answer these questions: What were the five biggest wins in my life? Does your current situation give you the most confidence and excitement? What are the five wins in the next season or year that would pose the biggest impact for you? That first question may be the most crucial one. It helps you positively frame your past and helps you selectively attend to the progress you are making. Most people focus on the pain, regardless of their success. They only see lack. They only see what they are not doing well—of course, having high expectations can be good for performance. But the persistent insistence that nothing is good enough is also bad for joy and even confidence.

In the Book of Philippians 4:11-13, Apostle Paul says,

"I have learned to be content whatever the
circumstances. I know what it is to be in need,
and I know to have plenty. I have learned

the secret of being content in any and every
situation, whether well fed or hungry, whether
living in plenty or want. I can do all things
through Him who gives me strength."

You can keep moving ahead in your life while enjoying the process at the same time. Showing that happiness and joy in Christ bolster motivation and success.

Sometimes in life, it is about risking everything for a dream no one can see but you.

5
BUILDING ON THE FOUNDATION

Establishing What You Have

A SENSE OF purpose at work can generate a feeling that what we do matters, but that is just the tip of the iceberg. The sense of meaning that employees derive from purposeful work translates into elevated levels of development in our society. One Writer wrote, "*Are you longing for more purpose in your work but have no idea how to get it? That sums up my entire 18-year corporate career. Purpose and meaning were continually elusive and impossible to attain, and I did not know why. Now, having transformed my corporate career, owning a business, practising as a therapist, and serving as a career counsellor, I understand why I was blocked from experiencing purpose and deep fulfilment in my work.*" Many lessons can be learned from the aforementioned Writer. Much cannot be said about this lesson, but the first thing we need to address to get on the path to experience more purpose in our work is to answer this: do you have a career or a purpose-driven in life? To put it simply and concisely, do you have a job or a calling? These are two distinct professional dimensions, and they are not at all the same. Thousands of people confuse them, and others want both at the same time. Many long for more purpose in their calling and yet have not done the internal or external work required to build that or the outcomes they are pursuing (which is impossible)!

On the other hand, a job can give you a resemblance of "security" and "stability" and might allow you to use your talents in productive ways, giving you the money to pursue your passion outside of work. A good job can bestow in many ways and give outcomes that matter to you. But it is not your calling. The calling chooses you (you don't choose it), and it will not let go. It compels you to contribute, achieve, fulfil and serve in ways that you often would never have initially imagined or thought of. In the end, you cannot go from a purposeless job that simply pays the rent and brings no joy or fulfilment to a tremendously meaningful one in one's field of influence. Before you claim your "purpose" and associate it with the work you do, you have to know what you love, care, desire, and about, what you have already created and why, and power up your commitment to bring more purpose into your life and work starting today, regardless of the challenges.

In my opinion, "purpose" can be defined simply as the motive, motivation, cause, basis and justification for the work you do. People longing for more purpose in their work are typical because they have made earning (or even advancement) the sole purpose of working. While money is important for most of us, millions of people—especially as they age and mature—find working solely for money for years upon years can end up feeling empty and unfulfilling purpose in life. If there's no compelling cause for the work except for making money, it can get old and feel lifeless to people. Most of us expect more from the work that takes up more hours than anything else in our lives. People often repurpose a skill set that they learned in college but never had a close connection with, so their work doesn't light them up or make them feel they are leveraging who they are genuinely in their work. The big question many people have thought about many years and on many occasions in answering to life fulfilment is that, ***"How do I ignite my purpose in life from my current job."*** If you long for a rewarding career that ignites passion within you, first, you need to get to know yourself better. Uncover your love, hate and strengths in life, the natural talents and skills you wish to use, the outcomes you care about and the kinds of people you respect and more.

Winston Churchill made a statement that is relevant to an individual's career. He said: ***"It's a mistake to try to look too far ahead. The chain of destiny can only be grasped one link at a time."*** It is ineffective, and you will end up making some big mistakes and missteps if you choose a career direction just by the vague idea or sound or look of it—to lay all your hopes of success onto just an idea that has never been tested for you. You must grasp the first link. I render that mistake as *"glomming onto the wrong form of a job or career before understanding the essence of what you want."* So many professionals tell me that they want to get rid of their current corporate careers and shift to being an author and write a bestselling book, work as a teacher, work in a non-profit, Become an actor or singer, Be a public (motivational) speaker, Work as a lawyer. The truth is, most of these people have no idea what the physical, living reality and identities of these jobs are, and be a fit. Secondly, you have invested plenty of time in your current career. Are you sure that chucking the entire baby out with the bathwater is what is right for you now, or are there just some elements you wish to walk away from and still have others that you could preserve that make you happy?

Start thinking profoundly about the **why** behind these desired roles that you admire. Do you want to act or sing because you deeply miss being involved in creative activities that brought you joy in your childhood? How much do you want to be a well-known author for your own sake, or because you want to bring a difference to the world? It's up to you to decide if you want to become a lawyer to make yourself a better person or you aim to help people struggling with challenges.

My challenge to you is this, look more deeply and uncover the **"essence"** of what you desire, and then start **"trying on"** new initiatives through small micro-steps, what I call (BUILDING ON THE FOUNDATION) that will enable you to experience that essence. Do not be exceedingly attached to how it has to look. Just continue to build upon the foundation—step by step, one brick after the other in a sequential manner. The first step is to take one small step toward doing something that lights you up, leads you to feel better about yourself, makes your heart beat faster. Engage in a pastime, a cause, or a class that makes you feel alive. Let go of the idea that this is your "job." Get out of your comfort zone and try something new that will allow your passion to grow from the inside. The truth is, no man worth his salt gives up without a fight, regardless of the circumstances. The **"imbalance of life fulfilment"** is a term I coined to describe the plight of many working people who have lost touch with the joy and passion that once drove them. To experience a greater sense of purpose, passion, reward, and impact in your professional life, you must first learn to prioritise your own needs and wants.

The 'Why' Behind Our Life's Fulfilment

MANY OF US can recall moments at work when a sense of meaning drove us—something that pushed us to go above and beyond the call of duty, to take on new, unexpected challenges without being asked to—that feeling can be elusive and vague. If you feel you have lost the motivation and satisfaction you once had, know that you are not alone in that dilemma. By perceiving yourself differently, you will discover what brings meaning and purpose to your work. It is sensible that losing what drives us in life fulfilment is so common if you think about it. As children, we do many things not solely because they naturally motivate us but also fulfil our satisfaction in life. However, as we grow older, we see ourselves through the lens of our college majors and first jobs. We learn a lot about what we do and how we do it as we advance in our careers, but we don't learn much about why we do it or what really motivates us in life. As we become less likely to work in the same position for the rest of our lives, we must know when we're shifting and drifting as we pursue our life's purpose. Understanding what motivates you is important, but it's not just about how it makes you feel.

Purpose drifting and shifting is when you connect what drives you with your potential goals, talents, capabilities, visions, strengths, and skills, using them as a basis for moving seamlessly from one opportunity to the next. When trying to find what motivates and moves us to chart a clearer course in life fulfilment, we are often told to write purpose statements and plans. While that sounds good, it could lead to frustration and disappointment when the wrong approaches are adopted. When we are not aware of our "why"—what motivates us or how to figure it out, we end up forgetting and losing those words as quickly as we wrote them down and kept them in our archives. The problem is that since we are so good at viewing our lives through the lens of our general college courses and our job programme pursued, we are clueless about how to pursue a broader view without the filters that brought us to where we are right now. What we need is a different strategy and approach, one that begins with first stepping outside of our limited imaginations and perspective, then searching the patterns that drive the reasons for what we do and implementing our why to our life fulfilment in a way that redefines us and clarifies our vision for our purpose.

Rediscovering What Drives Your Purpose

---

1. Find moments that matter. I've used this method with plenty of clients. To get a clearer picture of your motivations, you'll need to go from the broadest reflections on your life and work to the most specific ways in which you can apply it to your job. Consider moments in your life that stand out above the rest as a starting point. Moments like this are the most memorable because they elicit an emotional response from you when you think about them. Memories can be recollections of something you want, something you want to accomplish, someone you admire, or anything else that moves something in you. The things you want to leave behind may include what you want to say at your funeral, your inspirations, or a memory of when you felt alive.

2. Find what is meaningful. After discovering the moments that matter in life, you can now reflect on what has meaning to you by thinking about what things you care about deeply? What gets you satisfied and excited in your spheres of influence? And what is your inspiration in doing what you do—the motive behind what you do? What are you doing, and who you work with at these times? Is this a question that cannot be ignored? The key is to ensure broad and wide thinking about all aspects of your life.

3. Find What is Workless. To move even closer to what drives you, now ask yourself, what feels effortless and workless to you? When are you in the arena? Again, ensure that you are thinking about all the times throughout your life, not just recently and urgently, and you don't need to worry about where you were at the scratch. All you need is by building on the already laid foundation. My little experience as a coach is that when you open yourself to draw inspiration from all parts and times in your life, you get the most unfiltered and clear view of what motivates and drives all of what you do in life.

4. Discover the Power of Why. The next step on the proceed is connecting all of your reflections to find your way in life. You discover why by finding the pattern of what makes your moments that matter and the meaningful and workless actions you just evoked. There is always a pull—a reason we do what we do because everything has gotten a cause—knowing why we are drawn to what we choose and what we get from all of these experiences that stand out to our focus in life. For example, you may be driven by a desire to achieve a goal, solve a difficult problem, empower others by assisting them in reaching their full potential, or you may be motivated by the desire to contribute to a cause greater than yourself.

5. Strengthen Yourself. You need much stronger boundaries than we have today if you want to live an amazing and purposeful life. "Yes" and "No" must be learned for them to say yes and "no" in a way that doesn't upset others in the process. The need to separate from people and things that are draining them of their lives and time, and who don't believe in thrilling potential. And the need to start prioritising this journey of self-discovery and self-actualisation over so much else that you are engaged in is exhausting every day. If you cannot say "no" to what isn't working, you will be unable to say "yes" to things you want.

6. Gather them all together by looking at yourself from a different perspective; being that of your why you will discover what brings meaning and purpose to your life fulfilment. That is because you now have a complete image of not just how you use your talents and skills and push them effectively into the world; but also have now discovered or rediscovered your puling force, why what you do is so attractive—uncovering your patterns and your why is not a one-and-done exercise. Over time, the more experiences you gain, the more things will continue to focus. The more you adopt a habit of looking for the patterns in your work and life and why the clearer your drive and sense of life purpose will be.

6
UNLEASHING THE GREATER PORTION

The Portion Lived

SOMETHING IN your life purpose fulfilment, you need to burn bridges to stop yourself from crossing them again. Don't let the past be a reminder of what you are not in the present. The past is what taught you the lesson. The future is where you will apply the lesson. One cannot be both a victim and a victor at the same time. A successful king always leads to winning. Choose to be one or the other. Mediocre people, most of the time tries to be both and ends up being neither. Having low spiritual self-esteem and a sense of guilt will keep you locked up in the victim's prison. It will keep you in the past, rather than the future, of yourself (Christ). "In Him" means being a part of His life and future. Your past is not a part of God's plan for your future. Putting on the new man in Christ (the "new you") is difficult, but it is necessary. What we call "the new man" is what we call "the new you" for a "new future.**" God's grace can heal your past, present, and future all.**

Quantum Physics tells about a law that states that no object is unaffected by the observer. Meaning things appear the exact as you look at them. In other words, every observer uniquely sees a thing. If you see something as bad, it becomes so, and if you see it as good, so it becomes. Doubtfully, if you are bringing any negative from yesterday, which does not exist, then you are getting limited. Today you can, fix that broken pieces and change them. You can change your perception and manifest it today. Use your yesterday as a foundation to improve your today's roof. The stronger the foundation, the stronger the ability to withstand disturbances. Bill Keane once said, **"The past is history, tomorrow a mystery, so today is all we have. It's a GIFT; that's why it's called the PRESENT."**

In John 5, Jesus heals a disabled man and then direct him to pick up his mat and walk. Can our "mats" help us be thankful for and depend on God—even in fulfilling our lives purpose? *Then Jesus told him,*

> *"Get up! Pick up your mat and walk." At once,*
> *the man was cured; he picked up his mat and*
> *walked,"*
> *John 5:8-9*

"Pick up your mat." Why would Jesus tell the man to carry his mat with him after healing him? The man could not walk for the past 38 years, so maybe his mat must have been unpalatable, stinking, and terrifying. I have enjoyed watching Christ do amazing things in my own life and the lives of others, especially believers. However, if I had been the man in this narrative, I would have admired the miracle and then used my new legs to rush as far away from the filthy, ragged bed as possible. Jesus, on the other hand, urged the guy to take his mat with him. My problem with cleaning up that filthy mat is that once God forgives and cleanses me of my sins, I want to be free of any reminders of my old self to behold the manifestation of my new self in Him. I'm reminded of times in my life when I've wanted to run away from difficult situations—to leave "soiled" memories in the past and move on with my new life.

A story I once read about a couple during a particularly difficult season early in their marriage. It says, "My wife, Erin, and I was still learning how to handle conflict in healthy ways in our early state in marriage. We were having a furious disagreement one day when Erin asked for a time-out—a break to allow our emotions to calm down. But I persisted in forcing the conversation because I wanted to work through the problem and reconcile. Erin told me that she was unwilling to continue talking since the conversation seemed unsafe as I blasted past her attempted limit. Erin then entered our room and closed the door. I followed her in a futile attempt to terminate the quarrel. However, when I arrived at our bedroom door, it was locked. I was annoyed that I was now locked out of both the discourse and our bedroom. I pounded on the door numerous times, seeking to get entry—but it was locked. I was not sure who was more surprised by the sudden hole—Erin or me.

As I tiptoed back to the living room, I felt humiliated and disappointed in myself. Prior to this incident, In the midst of an argument, I had always been very proud of my ability to control my emotions and remain level-headed. Although I wasn't the enraged husband who punched holes in the house, my bedroom door suddenly had a large opening. This, I believe, jolted Erin and me back to reality, and we swiftly worked out our differences that day. I apologised several times for punching a hole in our door. After the incident,

I considered repairing the hole and even purchased the necessary tools, but I never did. I believe a part of me wanted to leave the hole as a reminder that I could achieve something I never imagined I could. In many ways, this story tells of how our past can influence our present moment and even the future to come as well. the hole in their master bedroom door served as his "mat." "The hole reminded me of my sinful nature and my need for God for the years we lived in that house. I had gotten reliant on my education and counselling skills to help me overcome the issues Erin and I were having. However, I needed to rely on God. When Erin and I fought, the hole humbled me and pushed me to seek God first. I'm not claiming that the hole magically ended our fights, but something happened over the next six months that had a beneficial impact on how I handled conflict with my wife "as the storey progresses

I ask, what are you running from, or what are you trying to forget? Maybe you are messing up in life, maybe your marriage has experienced infidelity, domestic violence, and unhealthy conflict, maybe you were addicted to drug or alcohol abuse, lying or deceit, or the withholding of affection or sex, maybe you are the person that all opportunities, potentials, and goals you have dreamt about—all had been violated and now living a life of emptiness, hopelessness, and frustrations. Whatever the weakness, God can use it for His ultimate glory. Instead of discarding the ugly "mat" aside, allow God to utilize your past to shape your future. It is not about what has gone astray, but rather, it is about allowing God to gather all the broken pieces and redefine them to outfit His purpose. The story of your life is a powerful reminder of God's ever-present help. The same is true in your life purpose. God is always present, and He can employ your painful experiences to shape you and redefine your priesthood into something amazing. Having faith means you have already believed and trusted that God has a great future in front of you and that He employs the past to train you for the future. In order to experience this great future, we have to align with Him. When I look at my life, I see pain, mistakes, and heartache. I see strength, lessons learned, and glorious potentials in myself when I look in the mirror. Though hard work doesn't make necessarily equity successful, hard work can beat talent.

The Utmost Portion

Apostle Paul says,

> *"I don't mean to say that I have already achieved these things or that I have already reached perfection. But I press on to possess that perfection for which Christ Jesus first possessed me. Dear brothers and sisters, I have not achieved it, but I focus on this one thing: Forgetting the past and looking forward to what lies ahead, I press on to reach the end of the race and receive the heavenly prize for which God, through Christ Jesus, is calling us."*

We often have attachments and feelings for the past. The past is hard to let go of, and it affects us emotionally. We most often give our past the power to define our future in many ways. How then can our past refine us rather than define us? How can it equip and inspire us to bring our best selves instead of destroying or deterring us from reaching our utmost purpose in life? So how do we let the past go, forgetting what is behind us so we can focus on what's ahead, the greater portion of our lives yet to be lived? How do we forget the guilt, what we have done, and what has been done to us? The remedy is that we can't change the past, but we can learn from it. Our past is a portion of our lives lived (a part of the whole, but not itself).

The past exists to train you, shape you, and prototype our new self to strive for more—more of the influence, more of our dominion, more of our potentials, more of our dreams and goals, more of our kingship and priesthood inside us, more of our visions and inspirations in our life fulfilment and to become who God wants us to become now.

There is a tale in the Old Testament reminding when the Israelites won against the Philistines in battle. For the Israelites, victory was not because of their military competence; it was because of God's phenomenon:

the Scripture says,

"But the Lord thundered with a mighty sound that day against the Philistines and threw them into confusion, and they were defeated before Israel."

After the battle, for honouring the divine victory by God,

"Samuel took a stone and set it up between Mizpah and Shen and called its name Ebenezer; for he said, 'this is how far the Lord has brought us."

Every time the Israelites encountered the stone, they were reminded of God's omnipresent help from their enemies. The disgraceful hole in the door of their house eventually became like an Ebenezer in his life—a reminder. The "hole in your door" and "your disgusting mats" can keep you relying upon God and grateful for His help in your dreams and goals. Instead of forgetting the past, it's better to use these painful experiences to strengthen your future.

7
CHANGE THE CAUSED, NOT THE LESSON

The Past is Dead

I HAVE DISCOVERED that in life fulfilment, you don't learn how to react; you learn how to respond. Self-control is strength, but calmness is mastery. You have to reach a point where your mood doesn't shift based on the insignificant actions of someone else. Allowing people to direct your life is not a good idea. Allowing your emotions to take control of your intelligence is not a good idea. It is better to feel the feeling, but not becoming the emotion is best. Witness it. Allow it. Release it. Les Brown once said, *"Forgive yourself first. Release the need to replay a negative situation over and over again in your mind. Don't become a hostage to your past by always reviewing and reliving your mistakes. Don't remind yourself of what should have, could have, or would have been. Release it and let it go. Move on."*

There will be many painful moments in your life that will change your entire world in a matter of time. A time in life where everything looks to have come to an end. A time where it seems you are only surviving on your last breath. A time where the last people in your life to look upon will finally wave you in the midst of the storm. These moments shall alter you. Let them make you smarter, kinder, and stronger to help straighten out that crown and keep it fitting and moving. Many are the challenges and moments of difficulties I have experienced in life, but regardless of all these struggles, I have never regretted my past; I only regret the time I have wasted with the wrong people who added no value to my life in those moments with them. Remember that life's most important lessons are usually learned at the worst times and from the worst possible mistakes.

The Bible describes God as being

"Able to do exceedingly abundantly above all that we ask or think."

and tells us that

"Nothing will be impossible."

With Him. There isn't a day when this isn't true. He is always capable of far more than we could ask of Him. Most of us tend to think little, pray small, believe small, and live small. "God may be able to do it for someone else, but not for me," we believe. This way of thinking hinders God's ability to work in and through us. It can also disallow us from unleashing our maximum potential in life.

That kingship and priesthood inside you is a liberation power and authority to do greater works. You are not voted into power as a king, so you cannot be voted out of power. You are being ordained as a king and a priest. So, make the laws, and they shall be established. No one can countermand your orders, and you have the power to negate your pronouncements. Set aside your decrees, and amend your statutes. Never call your past failures, disappointments, betrayals, struggles, separations, and retrogressions back to life; it is already dead. On this planet, the availability or scarcity of something determines its value. Gold and diamonds are valuable due to their scarcity. Similarly, because no one else is exactly like you, you are unique and irreplaceable. You are extremely valuable!

Gather Together with God

In (Matthew 16:24-26), Jesus was talking to His disciples and said this:

> *"If anyone desires to come after Me, let him deny himself, and take up his cross and follow Me. For whoever desires to save his life will lose it, but whoever loses his life for My sake will find it. For what profit is it to a man if he gains the whole world and loses his soul? Or what will a man give in exchange for his soul?"*

THIS PASSAGE is about submitting to Jesus, but it is also about your value. Jesus is saying that every person is more valuable than the whole world. Why? Because the earth as we know it will end, but people will live forever. You cannot afford to allow past failures, the thoughts, and opinions of others, or even the devil to make you feel devalued. Do not allow anyone or anything to convince you that your life has no meaning or purpose. Do not be fooled. What you've gone through has no bearing on your worth. It was—and continues to be—predetermined by God. The horrible things that have happened in your life are not a problem for Him, and they do not prevent you from realising your full potential. You are more valuable than the entire world.

(1 Peter 1:18-19) says,

> *"…you were not redeemed with corruptible*
> *things like silver or gold—but with the precious*
> *blood of Christ, as of a lamb without blemish*
> *and spot."*

All the world's wealth would not be enough to redeem you.

Jesus did not die for you to be valuable. For you, his death only showed your worth. You are still worth more than the entire world on your worst day. You must agree with God and see yourself in the same light that He does. *God told Jeremiah,*

> *"Before I formed you in the womb, I knew*
> *you; before you were born, I sanctified you; I*
> *ordained you a prophet to the nations."*
> *Jeremiah 1:5*

God is the one who scheduled your entrance into this world, and He has good things in store for you. Do not limit Him by trying to fulfil your destiny on your own instead of surrendering to Him. In the Scripture, we are informed that God's people "limited the Holy One of Israel." They witnessed Him part the Red Sea and walked through it on dry ground. They saw God drown Pharaoh and his entire army with their own eyes. Every morning, they received bread from heaven, and God even provided water from a rock. Even though they witnessed miracle after miracle, they limited Him.

What are the chances of that happening? But along the line, when the storms of the wave hit them as they journeyed on the wilderness, "They did not account His power." God desired to do so much more for them, and He intends to do more for you, too. But just like the children of Israel, you might limit God if you do not remember and rely on His power. It's a fallacy to bear repeating that potential is how far you can go in life without the presence of God. To travel where you've never gone before, to do what you've never done before, you need trust. Faith ties you to the power of God. No one can survive on yesterday's faith, and today's faith won't get you to where God wants you to go tomorrow. You must progress from one level of faith to the next.

Just as, without faith, it is impossible to connect with God, it is impossible to realize and maximize your full potential. Not even one person exists today whom God has not gifted. No one but Him knows the potential—the untapped power, dormant ability and unused strength— something is a part of you. This potential arrived in the shape of a seed. It requires development and growth. You'll never be able to ask God for more than He can provide. It's time to start dreaming greater dreams, praying bigger prayers, believing bigger dreams, and living bigger lives. It's time to fully surrender to Him, put your faith to the test, and realise and maximise your potential.

Maximizing the Dormant
Seed Inside You

SEEDS REPRESENT concepts that apply to both the natural and spiritual realms at the same time. When you begin to comprehend them, you will comprehend why things have occurred in your life and how to influence or change future outcomes. Too many Christians believe that God has predetermined what will happen to them in life. If God's will be done, I will live to be a senile older man, if only God knows. While God knows your future, it is incorrect to assume that you have no control over it. *When you read 2 Kings 20, you'll notice Isaiah, the prophet approaching King Hezekiah and telling him that the Lord has told him to do something.*

*"Set Your House in Order, for thou shalt Die
and Not Live!"*

The King is told what God has already told him will happen via the prophet of God, and these are the words of the almighty God. After King Hezekiah prays to God, God informs Isaiah to tell the King that he will live for another 15 years. If Hezekiah hadn't prayed, what would have happened? He would have perished as a result. Who changed the situation for Hezekiah to live 15 more years? God or Hezekiah. The truth is if a dormant seed is buried in the most fertile and productive soil (given all the necessary conditions—the land preparation process for soil treatment and preparation for production, best irrigation and drainage systems as well as fertiliser application), given all the time and money you have. In the end, you'll see that all your castles are built only in the air. The outcome will be the same as if the seed was simply buried and left to nature's mercy, or if the man never bothered to plant the seed at all because he was either wise or too lazy. But I'm not sure which is which. It's like asking a blind man to comment on your dress. Isn't it a little insane? *"Until the dormant seed has been treated to cure the seed of its dormancy, none of the germination elements will prove useful,"* any individual with knowledge of agriculture will confidently tell you.

Similarly, if a Christian does not establish or possess a real relationship with Christ Jesus, He's like a latent seed in the dirt, missing everything. While in the presence of the source of life, he will gradually rot to death. The truth is that it is those who seek and desire for God's presence who find Him, even in the darkest depths. If you are just following the Crowd, you are just one dormant seed in hardpan soil. Situations can be good or bad, things can work in your favour or against you, the path can be difficult or simple, and the list goes on. Farmers will, on occasion, rotate their planting schedules at the end of a growing season to help enrich the soil. On this plot of land, they've planted a crop. After being harvested at the end of that season, they till the ground, rough. It tills in the leftover plant material into the ground under it, aiding in the decomposition of the organic material and enriching and fertilizing the soil. This will aid in producing a greater and more fruitful harvest the next season. The goal is to make the plants grow bigger and faster by making them stronger and healthier. Tilling the dirt also disrupts the natural growth of bugs and other pests that would otherwise inhabit the region. The crop rotation process confuses the bugs and other pests, preventing them from gaining a stronghold on the type of crop that grows there. If a farmer plants the same crop each year, each consecutive year, it will get tougher to protect the plants from the bugs, and they will eventually kill off that vegetation.

Again, when a farmer ploughs the ground, it is tilled in rows that are typically against the flow of the wind currents. These are just a few of the gains of ploughing and crop rotation; there are many more. Ploughing is one of the initial steps in making the soil softer to receive a seed more easily. The seed, when germinated, grows its roots within the ground; a softer ground works better for that. *In the Book of Mark 4:4-8, Jesus told us about the parable of the sower. The verse says:*

"break up your fallow ground,"

indicating that it must have been tilled earlier. It (our hearts) must be prepared for planting. We are to purge our souls of all corrupt ideas, lusts, and desires—the weeds in our crops—and to have a broken and contrite spirit, full of sorrow and humiliation when we think of them. Then, and only then, we will be prepared to receive God's divine precepts—the seeds—so that they may take root and become deeply rooted in His Word? For doing (sowing) things that are agreeable to Him; for spreading His Words; for living a life that pleases Him; and for purging out of our lives those things that He cannot utilise and does not enjoy about us, God has a lot in store for us, lots of blessings, lots of rewards. The prophetic seeds lying dormant in your life are **about to come alive**. Make a difference right now by beginning to cultivate a personal connection with Jesus Christ. Desire to know Christ on a deeper level than the regular life you've been taught to live as a child. Stop chasing the crowd and get personal. Begin to act with reason and purpose (with your eyes on the prize) as you sincerely desire the growth of Christ in you. This is your season to go forth! Do not sit around and do nothing. Go forth and use the talents and abilities God has given you.

8
UNLEASHING THE HIDDEN TREASURES

The Unpredictable Cause

NEARLY ABOUT 2.0 billion of the world's population live in extreme poverty, meaning they lack the necessities of life. Necessities of needs and wants in life. A further 1.8 billion live at subsistence level, on a kind of "hand-to-mouth" existence that is only one crisis away from disaster. The tragedy is that economic poverty affects nearly 40 percent of humanity. So why is this the everyday reality of so many people in essence? This gives us a clear picture in the first two Books of Genesis about God's original intended purpose for us and communicates to us that is not how He wants His people to live. A fruitful and glorious life in Genesis chapter 2 is nothing but the worst in Genesis chapter 3 after the fall of man.

Good decisions would lead to provision and riches in a level and fair world, while poor choices would lead to poverty. The veracity of sayings like "In every toil there is profit, but mere chatter leads only to poverty" holds true in such a cause-and-effect environment. In a natural sense, laziness, wasteful indulgence, poor self-discipline, and addictive behaviour would lead to poverty and unsatisfactory life. And such is human nature at its worst. Hard labour, prudent spending, healthy self-discipline, and escape from addictions, on the other hand, would lead to prosperity and fulfilment in life.

This could be true for millions or billions of people worldwide today, with their relative prosperity or poverty owing to their own excellent decisions, hard effort, and innovation. Individual wealth and poverty may be the fair outcomes of personal effort and choice of a life lived in well-governed and developed societies, among those with equal access to education and resources, and in situations where illness, disaster, family dysfunction, crime, and accidents do not obstruct people's progress. But the truth is that we do not live in anything close to a level playing field on a global scale. The fallen world is neither just nor even-handed and such a tragedy. None of us starts life from the same position and on the same scale of reference. Our prospects in the world are heavily influenced by our environment, family, community, and societal and political conditions. Some of us were born into loving, nurturing homes in rich countries with diverse abilities and possibilities. Others, unfortunately, are born into situations that are resourceless in every way. They are never provided with the resources they require to live meaningful lives.

The majority of poverty is caused by some type of human error or sin. However, people's lack of provision or prosperity is not always due to their own wrongdoing. Poor governance, conflict, corruption, exploitation by the powerful, a lack of education and training, and family and social issues that hinder people from attaining their full potential contribute to many people not having enough, notwithstanding their own faults. In particular, lack of provision often occurs in whole or part with social or personal sin against the poor. i.e., they are victims of others' sins. A dictator seizes a family's land, depriving them of their capacity to farm or produce. A factory exploits poor workers by paying less than the legal wages and threatening those who object to such an offer. A wealthy landowner strips a large tract of forested land of vegetation, putting millions of people downstream at risk of flooding and famine. A husband gets addicted to gambling and abandons his wife and children to suffer pennilessly. We live in a world where an investment fails due to deception and fraud, leaving a family with no means to save for the future.

Other forms of poverty arise as a result of our planet's unpredictability. Natural disasters such as earthquakes, droughts, tsunamis, and floods can wipe out entire populations instantly, destroying crops, houses, possessions, and livelihoods. Even so, not all poverty is caused by sin, at least not sin that can be traced back to a specific person. Some persons cannot meet their basic needs due to a disability, disease, advanced age, or reasons beyond their control. In the Old Testament, three such groups of people were particularly vulnerable— "The widow, the orphan, and the foreigner." So many things are at play, some of which are within the individuals' control and others beyond their control. In this regard, the Bible is very practical. "Less than one-third of the proverbs dealing with rich and poor teach that people get what they deserve," according to one study, "while the rest recognise the presence and problem of socio-economic fairness." While there are times when the Bible links a lack of provision to a cause, Scripture is normally more concerned with the responsibility of those who have riches to care for those who lack provision.

A Promise of Real Treasure

WHEN STORIES about treasure hunting are presented in movies, literature, or television shows, the imagination is piqued. Ancient adventurers gathered gold, silver, and diamonds. Some of those treasures remain undiscovered to this day. There are, however, treasures far more priceless than anything found in a drowned adventurer's ship or a buried treasure box. The "self you" is where you'll find those treasures. We address them as, *"The promises of God and their value is beyond measure!"*

Fifty plus years ago, author David MacDonald wrote an article titled "Oak Island's Mysterious Money Pit." It related the narrative of Daniel McGinnis, a 16-year-old boy who went hunting on Oak Island in 1795. He discovered a 12-foot depression with a block and tackle suspended from a tree overhead the next day and returned with two buddies the next day to begin excavating. They came to a wooden board about 10 feet below. At 20 feet, they reached a second board, and at 30 feet, they discovered the third board. The boys gave up digging and returned to their farms, then returned to the site nine years later and started digging again in earnest expectation. They drilled a steel rod into the ground this time, which hit what they thought was a treasure chest about 95 feet down. But they could not reach the treasure; they returned to the site the next day and found the pit filled with water. It appears that whoever buried the riches employed advanced engineering techniques to construct flood tunnels above it to protect it from detection. According to one estimate, the sophisticated tunnel system on Oak Island would have taken 200 men up to two years to construct. McGinnis and his companions died before they could reach the riches. Since then, other treasure hunters have dumped millions of dollars into the "money pit" but have only found three gold chain links and a shred of ancient parchment.

Nonetheless, treasure hunters believe that incredible adventurer fortunes may be buried there. Some think the elaborate pit may hold precious treasure. Wealth seekers have spent their fortunes and lives searching for the treasure at Oak Island for more than 200 years. *According to legend, one treasure hunter said,*

> *"I have seen enough to know there is treasure*
> *down there and enough to know that no one will*
> *ever get it."*
> *Matthew 13:14*

> *"The Kingdom of Heaven is like a treasure*
> *hidden in the field, which a man found and hid.*
> *In his joy, he goes and sells all that he has and*
> *buys that field."*

Someone has buried a treasure and then died, according to the setting. The field's current owner is completely unaware of its existence. Somehow, the finder, a farm labourer, is entitled to it but cannot conveniently extract it unless he buys the field. This parable is thought to be about the tremendous worth of the Kingdom of Heaven and hence has a similar theme to the pearl parable. The "discovery" shows a "unique privilege," according to the good fortune. and a source of joy, but also reflects a challenge, just as the man in the parable gives up all that he has, to lay claim to the greater treasure he has found on the field.

One treasure hunt will always yield immense riches—if you are willing to dedicate yourself to the search. That treasure hunt begins in yourself, where we find wonderful treasures of truth and the priceless promises of God. *God has assured to give us eternal life, which is one of those wonderful realities. A young man in Matthew's gospel asked Jesus what he should do to inherit eternal life. Jesus answered,*

> *"'if you want to enter into eternal life, keep the commandments.' He said to Him, 'Which ones?' Jesus said, "'You shall not murder," "You shall not commit adultery," "You shall not steal," "You shall not bear false witness," "Honor your father and your mother," and, "You shall love your neighbour as yourself,"*
> *Matthew 19:17–19*

Jesus urged the young man to follow the Ten Commandments! *He listed the five of the Ten Commandments and then closed by quoting from Leviticus, in case anyone thought He was free to disobey any additional commandments not mentioned:*

> *"You shall love your neighbour as yourself,"*
> *Leviticus 19:18*

Here, Jesus demonstrated that the Ten Commandments are vital in our physical lives and our receiving eternal life from God. We should note that the Ten Commandments are not just prohibitions; the Fifth Commandment, telling us to honour our parents, *is even called*

"The first commandment with promise"
Ephesians 6:2.

Those who keep the Fifth Commandment will be blessed, according to God! Unfortunately, the young man in Matthew 19 *"went away sorrowful"* (v. 22) because he refused to heed Christ's commands. He was so enamoured of his "huge goods" that he couldn't see that he hadn't fully observed the Ten Commandments or Jesus Christ, who had given them to him.

Treasure hunters can spend a lifetime in search of fortune. But what good will it do them if they succeed? Will they follow in the steps of the rich young man in Matthew 19, who placed a higher value on his possessions than on his God? Jesus' disciples, on the other hand, are looking for an everlasting treasure: the Kingdom of God. Christians must seek God with an enthusiasm that rivals that of treasure hunters seeking wealth and diamonds. *Jesus said,*

"But seek first the kingdom of God and His
righteousness, and all these things shall be added
to you."
Matthew 6:33

Those in search of concrete, worldly wealth frequently fail. However, if we seek God's kingdom and righteousness, we shall discover the greatest treasure of all—and God also pledges to give us everything we require as a testimony of His love for us. We must, of course, play our role. We must "look for" and "knock." Are you looking for work? Yes, you should pray for a job. However, God may ask you to conduct some study and make some phone calls. Seek God's righteousness, and do what is righteous via God's Spirit. *God's Kingdom is compared to a priceless pearl in the Bible.*

> *"Again, the kingdom of heaven is like a*
> *merchant seeking beautiful pearls, who, when he*
> *had found one pearl of great price, went and sold*
> *all that he had and bought it"*
> *Matthew 13:45–46*

The pearl of great worth symbolises spiritual wealth and eternal life. Humans are continually learning the painful lesson that no amount of material wealth can bring permanent contentment. This can be seen in King Solomon's lessons. He had it all; *however, the concept of Ecclesiastes is repeated throughout the book:*

> *"Vanity of vanities, all is vanity."*
> *Ecclesiastes 1:2*

Solomon was the wealthiest man on the planet, but his riches did not bring him happiness. What did he come to after searching for happiness in so many different ways?

> *"Let us hear the conclusion of the whole matter:*
> *Fear God and keep His commandments, for this*

is man's all."
Ecclesiastes 12:13

As Christ taught and Solomon learned, true riches are available even to those who may be financially poor. Are you one of those who gives honour and attention to those with healthy bank balances while neglecting those in financial difficulty? Are you neglecting those whom God is honouring? *The Apostle James reminds us:*

"Listen, my beloved brethren: Has God not chosen the poor of this world to be rich in faith and heirs of the kingdom which He promised to those who love Him?"
James 2:5

God has promised His Kingdom to those who love Him, not to those who have vast material resources. Those who are wealthy in faith have true wealth—the true treasure—even though they are impoverished in this world's perspective. They're looking for God's plan for their lives. *As the book of Proverbs reads, God's method is a treasure.*

"My son, if you receive my words, and treasure my commands within you, so that you incline your ear to wisdom, and apply your heart to understanding; yes, if you cry out for discernment, and lift your voice for understanding, if you seek her as silver, and search for her as for hidden treasures; then you will understand the fear of the LORD, and find the knowledge of God. For the LORD gives wisdom; from His mouth come knowledge and understanding."
Proverbs 2:1–6

Those who receive the treasure of godly wisdom receive wonderful promises that can change their lives and eternity. *As the Apostle Peter penned:*

> *"Grace and peace be multiplied to you in the knowledge of God and Jesus our Lord, as His divine power has given to us all things that pertain to life and godliness, through the knowledge of Him who called us by glory and virtue, by which have been given to us exceedingly great and precious promises, that through these you may be partakers of the divine nature, having escaped the corruption that is in the world through lust."*
>
> *2 Peter 1:2–4*

"Expecting Great Things from God. Attempt Great Things for God."

ONEY TESTS our hearts like nothing else on earth. Whether the test of poverty or prosperity, money brings out the best and worst in us. Far too often, and I am sure you will agree with the fact that we do not know as much about God's view on money as we ought to but are afraid to admit. It's much more difficult to confront our financial shortcomings in Christian circles. Some people preach the (false) prosperity gospel, stating that God wants you to be wealthy. Some others preach the poverty gospel (which is likewise incorrect), claiming that God wants you to be poor. The reality is, everybody needs to continuously revisit biblical principles on money and be a balanced, lifelong student of financial stewardship. To help contrast some of the bad teachings, here are some starter principles to build upon.

Principle of God Owns Everything

WHEN WE think of wealth, we have to understand first that the earth is the Lord there off and that He owns everything! He does not owe you and me anything, He isn't stunned by the position of the earth, and He never

"lost the deed to the earth".
God does not just hold the deed to all land;
"He is the Creator of all land. He owns the cattle
on a thousand hills. "
Psalm 50:10

He owns everything under heaven, and for that matter, He is the owner of everything in regard. *The Psalmist declares,*

"The earth is the Lord's, and everything in it, the
world, and all who live in it,"
Psalm 24:1

There is no place for argument with the Bible on who owns everything. God does. What do we become if He is the proprietor of everything? We immediately discover that we are merely managers and stewards once we grasp this fundamental premise. We'll have to consider how we handled what He entrusted to our care one day.

Principle of Wealth Isn't Guaranteed on Earth

WHILE GOD owns everything, the Bible clarifies that wealth is not guaranteed for everyone on the planet. The impoverished, Jesus informed His disciples, would always be with them. We might deduce from His statements that people in this fallen and perverted world inevitably struggle financially. It's no surprise that Scripture emphasises the need of caring for the poor; they are among society's most vulnerable individuals (widows, orphans, the afflicted, the sick). Of course, this assumes they aren't poor because they are slackers. God is concerned about those who are in need. Because wealth is not always distributed evenly around the world, the book of Proverbs provides lessons on serving the poor. As a result, we should: Not oppress the poor, but rather be kind to them—Lend to the poor, and leave the outcomes to the Lord. —Be generous and share food with the poor—Give to the poor and not ignore them—Protect the rights of the poor. Caring for the poor is essential because wealth is not guaranteed for all. Beyond that, Scripture shows us what God wants for all of us. **Contentment and prosperity**, not riches, should be the goal of every believer. We must maintain a balance in our understanding of wealth and poverty. God accomplishes his purposes in and through the poor and the rich both. In the end, satisfaction is the key to happy life fulfilment.

Principle of Wealth is Not a Sign of Perfect Spiritual Status

"You have finally realized your full identity as a child of God when you step into the wealth God has for you, as many Prosperity preachers will tell you."

IT IS ESTIMATED that the Bible contains upwards of two thousand (2000) references to money. Approximately fifty percent of Jesus's parables dealt with stewardship of money and "stuff," and nearly three hundred (300) verses in just the Gospels alone deal with money. Does not this tell you that money and wealth are a very serious subject in the dealings of God? Moreover, not all of these verses convey exhilarating affirmations about money; rather, several contain cautionary statements about wealth. It takes plenty of discipline and biblical instruction to protect your heart from being drawn in by money's deceptions because it is often a diversion from what counts. The wealthy are often in a predicament between their affections for earthly things and the eternal life to come. By the power of the Holy Spirit, Wealthy believers can overcome temptations and use wealth as a tool for good. Still, there will certainly be a heart-to-heart conflict between gracious giving and the natural urge to keep, keep, and, more pridefully, the inclination to own, own, own. *Consider what the Bible says about money and make your own decision:*

Furthermore, the Bible gives special attention to the poor and afflicted when it comes to spiritual care, and they are often capable to worship more freely since they are free of the entanglements that come with wealth. The Book of Revelation wonderfully depicts this and informs us what ideal wealth is. The church of Smyrna is called "rich" by Jesus because, despite their poverty and sorrow, they have clung to their faith no matter what!

*They receive the highly esteemed crown of life for
their faithfulness and suffering on earth
Revelation 2:9-10*

The rich should be asking, **"How can I be more sacrificial?" Rather than, "How can I boast my elite status?"**

Principle of Wealth is a Tool for Gospel Advancement

EVEN THOUGH riches is not guaranteed on this planet, God does provide the opportunity to accumulate wealth. "No one handed me wealth—I earned it!" you might say. The children of Israel felt the same way, but Moses reminded them that God was rewarding them purely because of His sovereign will and purpose. If God has given you riches, you should thank Him sincerely and recognise that you have an important role in the advancement of His Kingdom. When it comes to wealth, the Bible is rather silent on what wealthy people should do with their wealth. Yes, leaving a legacy for your children is biblical and practical, and it is important to work hard and save for the future. But do you know what the most important goal of money is? To spread the gospel and fulfil God's will! Paul instructed Timothy that wealthy people should do the same. *He states, in a very clear sentence,*

"Command those who are rich in this present world not to be arrogant nor to put their hope in wealth, which is so uncertain, but to put their hope in God, who richly provides us with everything for our enjoyment.

Command them to do good, be rich in good deeds, and be generous and willing to share. In this way, they will lay up treasure for themselves as a firm

*foundation for the coming age, so that they may take
hold of the life that is truly life."*
1 Timothy 6:17–19

Investing in heaven is the best investing strategy on the planet! When Jesus stated to lay up treasure in heaven where nothing can damage it, He affirmed this investing plan. The truth is, Wealth gain is not a sin. You are allowed to enjoy it as a steward, not in the magnitude of ownership. But do not for a second fix your hope and trust in it. It's a tool for ministry in the kingdom advance, not materialism. Use your wealth to advance the gospel. You cannot take it with you.

Principle of Wealth is an Immense Responsibility

THE HARD truth we mostly deny ourselves is, "If you are wealthy, you were meant to build God's kingdom, not your earthly empire." Jesus instructed not to be concerned with material things but rather to seek His kingdom and righteousness and that everything else in life would be taken care of. With whatever resources we have, we are all called to live generous lives. When a widow gave two cents, Jesus remarked she had given more than the wealthy who gave vast sums of money. He does not see the size of your gift; He sees the state of your heart. And that is the distinction. When we give, we must do so gladly and not under duress. Wealth is a stewardship obligation, trusting that God has blessed you to be a blessing and that He will keep blessing you as you are accountable for whatever has previously been entrusted to your care. Our job is to work hard, invest wisely, and give freely, not to keep. There are many hurting and broken people in the world, and money can make a huge difference in ways that will last a long time. You will be held responsible for how you handled the wealth that God has bestowed upon you. That is a huge burden to bear. What will your discourse be like in front of Christ's throne? Will you stutter and stammer, claiming to have attempted to donate a little here and there while spending the most of your money on your pleasures and allowing the needy and the church to suffer? Or would you joyously report to the Master, saying, "Lord, giving sacrificially for your work went against the grain of this world at times, yet pleasing you was the priceless treasure I hung on to!" "Well done, good and faithful servant!" I'm sure we'll hear if we live that way. I'm going to put you in control of a lot of things because you've been faithful with a few things. Come and share in your Master's joy!" Wealth is a responsibility, not a fault. Make the most of it.

9
THE PRINCIPLES OF FAILING TO FAIL

The Wisdom to Deal with Failure

THERE ISN'T one out there who hasn't failed—some perhaps more than others. The Bible recognizes that humans do fail: We all stumble in many ways in search of life fulfilment. But the paramount thing is how we handle our failures. Everyone aspires to be successful. I've never encountered somebody who set out to be a failure on purpose. This is, without a doubt, why so much has been published about "How to Be a Successful Person in Life" and why these articles, books, and magazines are so popular. It was Theodore Roosevelt, I believe, who stated, **"The only person in life who never makes a mistake 'fail' is the person who never does anything."**

The core reality is that failure is one of those ugly and unpleasant realities of life—a common experience to all of us in some sense. Thus, handling failure in various forms and degrees is a vital part of the spiritual life and another sign of maturity and dominion. The fear of failure is being scared of not accomplishing the desired goals and ambitions in life. Fear of failure might lead people to sabotage their efforts to avoid the possibility of a bigger failure, missing a greater opportunity, or avoiding trying something extraordinary. Many people are afraid of failing at a certain point in their lives. It can render them immobile—prevent them from moving forward ever in their lives. And such is a life catastrophe.

A comprehensive examination of the Bible indicates that most of the Bible's great people failed at some point, but that failure did not prevent them from reaching their full potential for God. This was true of Noah, Abraham, Moses, David, Elijah, and Peter, and it was a chronological and partial list. Though they failed at some time, and often in substantial ways, their efforts not only recovered from their failures, but they also used them as a vehicle for growth—they learnt from their mistakes, confessed them to God, and were frequently able to be used in even more powerful ways later in their lives.

The way a leader handles failure will have a tremendous impact on his future ministry. One could have reasoned that Peter's failure in the judgement hall had permanently shut the door for leadership in Christ's kingdom. Instead, the breadth of his repentance and the sincerity of his love for Christ reopened the door to a new domain of impact.

"Where sin abounded, grace did much more abound,"

as the Bible edifies us. A study of Bible figures suggests that the vast majority of people who shaped history were guys who failed at some point, some of them spectacularly yet refused to stay in the dust. Their failure and remorse provided them with a more expansive understanding of God's grace. They learned to know Him as not only the God of the second chance but in content, the God of many chances to His children who had repeatedly failed Him.

I once read in an article, "Maria describes her relationship with food as a love/hate affair. Food is her secret companion, her lover, and her (Best Friend Forever). On the way to work, during every work break, at lunchtime, on the trip home, at dinner time, and after midnight hugging, she loves to organize special times with her favourite meals. While she is eating, she savours every delicious morsel. However, once the meal is in her stomach, she starts to dislike it. She despises the fact that she has no control over her eating. She despises the fact that she has gained 10 pounds and feels bloated. She despises the fact that she has failed yet another diet. She understands that she must change her disordered eating, but she is afraid of failing once more. —the proceeding article is ongoing in the next three paragraphs." I have discovered these three deceptions that contribute to the fear of failure in life fulfilment.

- People-pleasing
- Perfectionism
- Pessimism

People-Pleasing

People-pleasing is the fundamental cause of the fear of man to fail. *The Bible states,*

> *"The fear of man lays a snare."*

The fear of becoming a failure often controls and confines a person's thoughts and actions (the killing of the "I can do spirit in you"). "Maria is keen to impress her relatives during the Christmas family reunion by demonstrating that she has shed the weight she gained after having two children. She chooses to go on a crash diet since she is afraid of what others may think or say. She doesn't stick to the diet, doesn't lose weight, and decides not to attend the Christmas family gathering."

Perfectionism

At its foundation, perfectionism is a matter of pride. It will not accept anything lesser than perfection as a standard. People with this mindset have exorbitantly high standards, strive for perfection, and are harshly critical of themselves and others who fall short of their expectations. Perfectionism's fear of failing leaves a person useless and hopeless in life. This is deception at its cost because God's *Word indicates to us,*

> *"For all have sinned and fall short of the glory of*
> *God,"*
> *Romans 3:23*

"Maria makes an appointment with a nutritionist. At the first meeting, Maria sees that the nutritionist is a little pudgy around the waist. Immediately, Maria is turned off to whatever information is given and leaves the appointment determining never to return. She fears failing to eat right because the nutritionist did not live up to her expectations."

Pessimism

Pessimism is fearing that whatever is destined for in life will not happen. There is no optimism or promise for the future. Pessimists have a "glass-half-empty" perspective when it comes to problems. They refuse to believe in the best-case scenario and have no positive aspirations. This is a serious problem that comes not only within the heart but from the mind as well. The Psalmist yells to himself, "Why are you cast down, O my soul, and why are you in turmoil within me?" His faith wrestles with his fear in anguish. There is a sense of sadness for the future. "Maria is pessimistic about the weight loss program at work. She has no confidence that she will lose weight. She has tried so many different diet programs resulting in nothing but utter failure. She thinks to herself, "Why would this program be any different? I will fail at this too."

The Backdoor Principle

DO YOU HAVE the same fear of failure as Maria? Admitting and facing your fear of failure takes guts. Are your fears motivated by a desire to please others, perfectionism, or pessimism? A favourite hymn for many believers is "Victory cometh from the Lord" because there is victory in the Savior. This is because believers are super-conquerors in Christ. Other Bible visions translated it as "Absolute Victory". Significantly, this statement by Apostle Paul is made in a context that considers the reality of the varied attacks of life, which must include failure. The historian Froude wrote, **"The worth of a man must be measured by his life, not by his failure under a singular and peculiar trial."** Peter the Apostle, through forewarned of Jesus' arrest but thrice denied his Master upon the first alarm of danger; still that Master, who was aware of his nature in its strength and its infirmity, selected him. Their failure is not the end of an effective life with and for the Lord, provided they understand God's wonderful grace and incredible forgiveness and acceptance through Christ. While there may be aftereffects to live with (as David did) and severe challenges to go through, the mature believer relies on God's grace for speed, strength, growth, and insight and uses failure as a doorway to reach their full potential.

"Who will be able to separate us from Christ's love?" Will there be tribulation, suffering, persecution, starvation, nakedness, danger, or death? As it is written,

> *"For your sake, we encounter death all day long;*
> *we were considered as sheep to be slaughtered.*
> *No, in all these things, we have complete victory*
> *through him who loved us, for I am convinced*
> *that neither death nor life, nor angels, nor*
> *rulers, nor things that are present, nor things*
> *to come, nor powers, nor height, nor depth, nor*
> *anything else in creation will be able to separate*
> *us from the love of God in Christ Jesus our*
> *Lord,"*
> *Romans 8:35-39*

Many a time, we often speak of the **victorious** life after a trial or a test. Nonetheless, there are many flaws in life because none of us will always appropriate the triumph over sin that Christ has won for us on the cross. We don't like to admit it or talk about it, yet there are numerous setbacks. Naturally, as significant and painful as it is, this form of failure pales in comparison to a spiritual failure, such as David's sin. While David was able to recover from his sin and was still used by God; as a result, there were long-term effects in his and others' lives. Failure is the truth of life for the believer's community, but God's grace is more than adequate to overcome any situation.

The Prevailing Attitude Principle

WE KNOWINGLY or unknowingly ignore our sins and failures because admitting them is to admit failure, which is a plague worse than death. Currently, bookshops are brimming with popular "How to Succeed Manuals" on every subject imaginable. And why is it the case? Because we are so preoccupied with God's glory? I hope so, but there are other factors at play. It's because we look at failure with scornful eyes all too often. Failure is viewed as a Waterloo for us. We regard it as the pest of all plagues and the worst thing that could ever happen to us. As a result, many people are neutral, immobilised, or playing the cover-up game due to their fear of failure. For fear of failing, people often refuse to take on a task or accept responsibilities. Many people assume that if they fail, they will be as bad as the failure. They believe that failure equates to being a horrible person and a failure. However, as previously stated, most of the great leaders in Scripture had a lineage of failures at some point during their lives.

Adam and Eve failed to obey God and ate from the forbidden tree. Abraham fled to Egypt because of the drought, although he should have stayed in the land and trusted the Lord. And this was far from the last of Abraham's misfortunes. In an attempt to assist his people, Moses got ahead of the

Lord and murdered the Egyptians. Later, in his rage, he smote the rock against God's instructions. When he should have been fighting, David stayed at home, committed adultery with Bathsheba, and then plotted the death of her husband. Despite his self-assurance and boastfulness, Peter denied the Lord, as did the rest of the disciples who fled before our Lord's imprisonment was completed that evening.

A basic principle applies here. God must engineer failure in us sometimes before He brings about success for us **(out of the carcase may come something sweeter).** If we learn from our mistakes rather than crawl in the dirt, our failures are often rungs on the ladder of growth. This isn't meant to justify sin or put a priority on failure or blunders. This does not connote that a person must face failure before succeeding or fulfilling the purpose, but our failures, either in the form of rebellion or mistakes, can become tools of learning and stepping stones to our realm of success and life fulfilment. The point is, we should never let our fear of failure paralyze us from doing something that challenges our comfort zone; neither should we let our past failures keep us down or keep us from recovering and moving forward in the service of the Savior. Meaning that we should never allow failure to make us think of ourselves as a failure or that we can never amend or that we can never again account for the Lord, or that God cannot do anything for us because we have failed in a certain way. The Scriptures says we are all sinners and prone to failure, but in Christ, we can become overcomers. I have learned that in life fulfilment, *"We must expect reverses, even defeats. They are sent to teach us wisdom and prudence, to call forth greater strength and speed, and to prevent our falling into greater disasters."*

The Advancing Attitudes
Principle

WE MAY HAVE to live with the consequences of some of our failures or sins, but God is free to love and use us for His purposes because of grace to use our failings as opportunities for growth and progress. We must admit that this principle cannot be compromised in any way so far as failure is concerned. The understanding that failures remind us of the consequences of our decisions—reaping what we sow will help us advance our way of doing things. This is the law of the harvest. Failures prompt us of what can happen, they can make us care, but they should not be allowed to paralyze us. We recognize that our failures show us what we should and should not do; they become lessons in where we went wrong and always ask why we went wrong. It can help us prevent making the same mistake twice if we learn from our past experiences. Let us critically examine the life of Thomas Edison: A prodigy in the late 1800s and early 1900s. Thomas Edison invented the incandescent light, the storage battery, the microphone, the phonograph talking movies, and more than 100 other things. December 1914, he had worked on a storage battery for ten years. This had greatly strained his resources. This particular evening, spontaneous combustion broke in the film room.

All packing materials, celluloid for records and film, and other flammable items were engulfed in flames within minutes. Fire departments from eight nearby towns responded, but the heat was so high, and the water pressure was so low that putting out the fire was impossible. Everything was wiped out. Edison died at the age of 67. With all of his assets exploding in flames. He was 67 years old, no longer a youthful man, and everything was on fire. The next morning, Edison looked at the remains and said, **"There is great value in disaster. All our mistakes are burned up. Thank God we can start new."** Three weeks later, Edison managed to deliver the first phonograph. This teaches us great lessons that great influential people never accept failures and defeats in life. Acknowledging your failures and refusing to hide behind any lame-duck excuses. Confess any sin to God when it is involved in failure. Study and examine what happened so you can learn from the failure. Put it behind you and advance. When we respond to our failures as tools for growth and greater degrees of confidence and commitment to God, rather than rebelling and being hardened by the hardship, we can always turn them into tools for growth and higher levels of trust and commitment to God.

The Fallacious and Misleading Principle

G RACE, NOT performance, determines our acceptance of the Lord. We are human; therefore, we are not and will never be flawless. Our lives are still in God's hands. God's work is not done with us yet; hence, we need to continue with His plan. According to the teachings of Scripture, some people have truly failed. We have failed in our role to influence if we do not understand why we believe what we think and then fail to provide a sufficient justification to those who inquire about our hope. That may be a stepping stone to better equipping ourselves and becoming more assertive in our impact, but there was a failure there. There is false guilt of failure because of a wrong view of success. Many missionaries have dutifully laboured in foreign countries without seeing many converts, but this does not mean they were failures. In this content, the Prophet Isaiah is a crucial instance. Right from the start, after seeing the Lord high and raised, admitting his and his nation's sins, and saying, "Here am I, send me," God sent him to preach to a people who would not listen and warned him about it. He was a failure in the eyes of the world, but not in the eyes of God. A different type of failure exists for those who falsely feel they are successful! These Christians may make a decent living and contribute greatly to the body of Christ. They perceive themselves to be role models for others, either unconsciously or intentionally. They are unaware, however, that they are failures in God's eyes. One man put it this way: **"I climbed the ladder of success only to discover that my ladder was leaning against the wrong wall!"** Heaven shall be full of delights! Many "successful" Christians will be nobodies in the kingdom, while others whose lives have been strewn with the debris of failure after failure will be magnificent. People apply a variety of false and misleading notions about success to themselves and others, yet they are all distortions of the truth.

Most of these are based on some type of faulty comparison that has no basis. To those who did this kind of foolishness, *the Apostle Paul wrote in 2 Corinthians 10:12; EMPHASIS ADDED,*

> *"For we would not dare to classify or compare ourselves with some of those who recommend themselves. But when they measure themselves by themselves and compare themselves with themselves, they are without understanding."*

Comparing ourselves to others causes this misperception. We should all do our best with the abilities God has given us, and we have every right to look to others for examples of Christ-like character. But this is not the same as comparing ourselves to others based on their gifts, abilities, money accounts, belongings, status, and other such criteria, and then attempting to assess our own or someone else's success or failure based on such comparisons. Others define their success in terms of their bank accounts and the luxury objects they can afford—furniture, automobiles, a large home, yachts, and so on.

Lutzer once said, if money is a basis for judging success or failure, it is obvious that Jesus Christ was a failure! Consider this: when Christ needed to pay taxes, He told Peter to look for a coin in the mouth of a fish. Why? He was without a coin of His own. Most of us would be shocked if our children were not delivered in a modern hospital or enrolled in the best school possible! When He (Jesus) died, the soldiers divided His robe into lots. That was everything He had in the way of worldly possessions. He died in a state of nakedness and emptiness. Was Jesus Christ a flop? If money is the yardstick by which He is measured, then yes. The foxes have their holes, and the birds of the air have their nests, but the Son of Man had nowhere to call home. Earning money, and even preserving some, is, of course, legal and important for the kingdom's control and prosperity. But what we earn is not a measure of God's blessing. And I might add, wealth and possessions are never evidence of success in God's viewpoint. Many wealthy people are failures from God's perspective. The idea is that the presence or lack of money is not indicative of success or failure in and of itself.

The comparison game pervades practically all aspects of life. It may entail comparing pals, i.e. name-dropping, to imply that one is successful because he hangs out with the appropriate crowd. It could also involve Christians comparing the size of their church, the budget of their mission, the number of publications released, and so on. None of these things is sufficient evidence of success in God's eyes. In this scenario, a perfect illustration is when Moses struck the rock when God had told him to only speak to the rock. Water flowed. The people were jubilant and satisfactory! Was Moses a success? **Yes, in the eyes of men. No, in the eyes of God!** It was His disobedience that brought water, but it also brought punishment. Results in themselves are not proof that God is pleased. It is possible to win attendance contests, disseminate the Gospel, and see results; all these activities can be done without pleasing God! Such results can be achieved by deceptive promotions or for purely personal satisfaction. It is not enough just to do God's work; it must be done according to His way and for His glory.

10

OVERCOMING THE INVISIBLE DEVICES

Be a Kingdome Builder

JESUS CHRIST'S principal message was the Kingdom of God. It was the subject on which he spoke, instructed, and offered more instructions than any other. Unfortunately, many Christians struggle to grasp what the Kingdom of God entails and how it should affect their daily lives. I have discovered how our understanding of the Kingdom of God as kings and priests directly affects the nature of every believer's mission and purpose, establishes new levels of spiritual authority and supernatural power, and allows us to live a life that brings influence and transformation into every area of our world. A step-by-step guide loaded with powerful and practical keys to help you activate and release kingdom culture in your relationships, workplace and profession, church, neighbourhood, city, and nation, enabling you to see God's will be fulfilled on earth as it is in heaven.

In one of Jesus's Powerful Parables, He described the kingdom of His Father by comparing it to yeast.

"The kingdom of heaven is like yeast, which a woman took and hid in three measures of meal till it was all yeast."
Matthew 13:33

I would like to dwell on this illustration that Jesus used

(baking); as a basis of Him most likely seeing His mother do when growing up. It signifies a lot about us and what happens when we live our lives in accordance with the Kingdom of God. It all starts with a single step: the yeast was small, transforming the entire dough. People who have dedicated their lives to Jesus are the foundation of the Kingdom of Heaven. God places us in various regions and situations so that we might influence and transform our surroundings, society, and mindset. The Kingdom is concealed, operating from within; it is not visible but very active. It is not for us to retain it for ourselves but to share it with everyone. When the tree has grown to the size of a mustard seed, the branches will have nests for the birds of the air to come and rest. Our influence will pull people to what we bring, not to ourselves so that they can find a place to rest and live-giving them a piece of His kingdom. Everyone has the ability to influence others. We all have an impact on someone. God expects us to be dutiful stewards of that power for the sake of His kingdom. Our influence is given to us, not for our own selfish gain, but so that we might communicate the good news about him to build the Kingdom. I will be held eternally responsible for how I used the power that God has given me in this life. How I use my influence in the transient world has eternal consequences, as the Bible demonstrates. In His judgement, God will ask every human being, "What did you do with my Son, Jesus?" And He will ask everyone in His household, "What did you do with the time, resources, and influence I provided you?"

How Influence Advances

THE TERRITORY of a kingdom is reflected and magnified by the cities of the king or the priest that have an active treasury (population and wealth) in them. The more inhabitants these cities have, the greater the influence on the surrounding fields. The further away from a field, the more the influence will be reduced. If a king or a priest has several cities, the influence will multiple. A city's influence has a maximum range, which is dependent on the size of that city. In other words, to increase the scope of your influence, you have to get more population in your cities. In the Book of Ecclesiastes, Solomon is very aware of the invisible devices of influence. This influence can be either for good or evil. One wise person can save a city.

On the contrary, 'one sinner destroys much good.' A human being can employ their influence for evil and cause great harm. The influence does not need to be as great as these tyrants, oppressors, and persecutors to have an unbearable effect. Dead flies in perfume make it stink, and a little foolishness decomposes much wisdom. If even a dead fly can impose a bad influence, then the least influential human being can indeed influence evil or good. We can all be a fly in the ointment!

Paul is deeply aware of his influence as a Christian and, particularly, as an apostle. He is determined to maximise his influence for good and to put up with anything rather than hinder the gospel of Christ. He appears to regard his call to singleness as one of the ways he can increase his power. He isn't implying that anything is amiss with the relationship. The other apostles, including 'the Lord's brethren and Peter,' appear to have all been married. Paul is zealous in his preaching of the gospel. He doesn't want anything to go in the way of it having the greatest possible impact. As a result, he doesn't use any of his rights because his purpose is more important. He is compelled to preach. He writes, "Woe to me if I do not preach the gospel!" He is simply conducting an obligation that he feels. He wants more than anything that people should be able to hear the gospel free of charge. He would rather die than be stripped from the opportunity to preach the gospel free of charge. Another way he tries to increase his clout is to work a second job to supplement his income. He is quick to remind out that he is not required to do so: "*The Lord has commanded that those who preach the gospel receive their living from the gospel*" In other words, as Christians, we should financially support those who spread the gospel full-time. Paul argues that although he had this right, he did not claim it. We've decided to put up with anything rather than get in the way of or detract from the Gospel message. Apostle Paul in these cases was more careful about the invisible deploy devices of the devil to sabotage him in his ministry.

Kings Rule by Invasion of Territories

"For the weapons of our warfare are not carnal but mighty in God for pulling down strongholds, casting down arguments and every high thing that exalts itself against the knowledge of God, bringing every thought into captivity to the obedience of Christ, and being ready to punish all disobedience when your obedience is fulfilled,"
2 Corinthians 10:4-6

The devil affects people's attitudes by moving our reasoning processes toward satisfaction of the self. He gives disinformation and stirs up our spirit. Here is what is so perverse about this: It is not evil for one to take care of himself. What is evil is to make our satisfaction more important than God's or others. We are to serve God before anything else (the great commandment), and the second is like this—we are on an equal par with others physically. God gives us no right or privilege to make ourselves better or more important than God or other human beings anywhere in the Bible. We can see where the adversary is trying to lead us—to the point when self-satisfaction takes precedence over complying with what God says is the limit of our authority.

To put it another way, he will encourage us to elevate ourselves above righteousness and truth. To adopt a friendly, familiar attitude toward the world is to get along with God's adversary. In more pragmatic terms, what does a friend of the world mean? It is to adopt the worldly set of values and desire what the world wants instead of choosing divine standards or revelations. In other words, if a person does so, he has rendered himself vulnerable to the devil's hidden devices, for Satan is the world's ruler! We are committing a mistake if we choose the path of the world. The worldly individual will nearly always opt to gratify his desires and act on them, resulting 0in turmoil, conflict, and war. It can't be any other way because the world's spirit is Satan's spirit, and laws are in effect that will generate what they're designed to produce. That was the issue with the congregation, according to James. If some other apostle had been writing it, such as the apostle Paul did in I Corinthians 3, he would have written, *"You are yet carnal."* These were converted folks who were still sensuous, as evidenced by their choices. It wasn't that they didn't have the Holy Spirit, but that they were still spiritually deficient. They chose to rely on their character, understanding, information, and vision from the outside world, demonstrating that Satan was still in control of their lives. A sequence of texts will be read to emphasise the dangers that the world poses to us. *The apostle James writes:*

> *"Adulterers and adulteresses! Do you not know that friendship with the world is enmity with God? Whoever, therefore, wants to be a friend of the world makes himself an enemy of God".*

These folks aren't lost, according to James. He's warning them that they're moving in that route since they've previously been unfaithful and are now backsliding. The globe is the unspoken but obvious cause of their being drawn back as if it were the tempting temptress. We cannot straddle the line between God and the world, according to James. He's elaborating on the concept that "no one can serve two masters." This war is framed by these two relationships—God and the world—as a black-and-white issue; there is no grey area in this conflict. It is impossible to remain devoted to God while pursuing self-centred, worldly desires.

Apostle Paul continuous to provide another guiding principle to hold dear:

> *"But God forbid that I should boast except in the cross of our Lord Jesus Christ, by whom the world has been crucified to me, and I to the world."*

This exemplifies Paul's spiritual development and outlook on his interaction with the world. In terms of any relationship he has with the world, the world is dead and crucified, and he is as well. It's full of colourful visuals. How much wilful dedication can one have in a relationship that isn't working because both sides are "dead" to each other? Paul had renounced the whole worldly system. It no longer appealed to him; in effect, he was dead in relation to it. However, the world's pressure never ends. *The Bible says,*

> *"Do not be conformed to this world." The Greek more correctly reads, "Stop allowing yourself to be fashioned to the pattern of this age,"*

or to puts it in a more precise way, *"Don't let the world around you squeeze you into its mould."* This is the risk we face when we let the world become too important to us. *"It is better to be forewarned than to be forearmed."* The world gently but relentlessly coerces us into conforming to its way of thinking, value systems, and, as a result, attitudes, and behaviour. If we are vigilant and properly guarded against the infiltration of worldly attitudes and behaviours, we will soon be able to recognise when others revert to following the world's path. The tenacious influence of the world is real as the devil, the god of this world, is its driving force. These forces are invisible devices serving as a medium through which he spreads his propaganda and disinformation. He intends to manipulate humanity by confusing people about what to believe. Due to this Satanic effort, we are apt to become misinformed, lackadaisical, disinterested, and discouraged even though we are converted. We must be aware of it and resist it.

When a person encounters Babylon's ways and language and fails to check the attitudes, he picks up and lives; a more elusive influence happens. Above all, men must cope with Babylon's invisible deity and leader, the prince of the power of the air, and his legion of equally invisible demons, whose spiritual communication is inaudible but alluring and strong. Resisting it can be overwhelming even for those aware of this communication; it calls on one to be constantly on guard. Nonetheless, the secret to stifling Babylon's siren song is to oppose communication. God warns us to leave her, but there is nowhere to go! Satan's influence is felt all across the world thanks to Babylon's communication capabilities. Because this world's deity and his assistants have been permitted to speak with and deceive mankind, the apostle John reveals in Revelation that we have nowhere to flee. *"So, the great dragon was cast out, that serpent of old called the Devil and Satan, who deceives the whole world; he was cast to the earth, and his angels were cast out with him."* We are born into this ready-made, deceived world, take it for granted, and absorb it until God reveals an alternative. Faith does not render things easy; it makes them possible. When you have done everything you can do, that's when God will step in and do what you can't do. Compared to previous Babylon's, the major difference in what we now face in modern Babylon lies in its communication's intensity, availability, and receptivity. As far as we are aware, mankind has never been confronted with such perverted, persuasion-based demonic powers as he is now. In addition to entrenched systems of thought and standards of behaviour, they now have global access to the visible and auditory influence of radio, music, movies, television, and the Internet. There is nowhere to flee. Then, the battle to resist is almost entirely internal - it is fought right where we live as we rule as kings and priests by invasion into these demonic territories to overpower them.

11
SACRIFICE OF ALIGNMENT

The Challenge

EVERY HUMAN shall be tested – Adam, Eve, Abraham, Moses, David, Peter, Paul—*You as well as me so that David can write in his Psalm 139,*

"Search me, oh God, and know my heart, test me...."

Those who pass those tests, which are always tests of our devotion to God, are authentic. And a legitimate life, one that has been tested in the fire and does not say or repeat hollow and cheap words, becomes authentic and therefore convicting. Words can persuade, but only a life supported by God can convict. Because no one lives in a vacuum, such a life cannot remain concealed and unseen. In the six fundamental realms of life: family, education, communication, culture, business, and politics, it is tangible and authentic. And these are the six places where God's influence will be seen and difficult to ignore for anyone.

Many people today claiming to be Christians are caught playing outside the Kingdom, God's governmental structure, because they do not respect or obey His official rules? *We'd spot them right away if they didn't have any blessings:*

> *"No fruit that lasts, no multiplication, and no
> world impact"*
> *Genesis 1.22, 28*

We shall see a return of fruitfulness, multiplication, and a movement that quickly spans the entire globe with God's blessing, keeping the laws and respecting God's blueprints for life, church, sex, money, and power. This will be an actual, heavenly power movement. But only if we are not just loved and graced, but also blessed, can this happen.

The essence of the Kingdom of God is the domain of his uncontested rule. And why would anyone do such a thing, kneeling in front of a king, voluntarily, freely, out of his own choice, without being forced with a gun to his head? The answer is simple as it is powerful. Love! God loves us; we are invited to love him back. We then fall hopelessly and madly in love with the family of the King, our new family, with one another. And together, we love the world, in self-sacrificial service, and do anything that it takes to introduce them to our King. Whenever a king is found, he becomes his lawful subject. As a top priority in life, such a person now respects the King, his values and principles—the kind of valid justice before Him, His righteousness, and His kingdom-law. Nothing can compare to the role that Jesus the King now plays in the lives of a new royal subject. A person who is faithful to Jesus as King stands out like a fish swimming against the flood in a world where everyone wants our loyalty—patriotism, religion, clans, tradition, money, power, supermarkets, fun, political doctrines, tithe-collecting churches, systems, and gurus of all kinds. Legitimacy is the product of such devotion. Why? Because only loyalty that has been tested and proven leads to credibility. When it comes to loyalty, it's cheap if it doesn't hold up when tested.

Nobody gives a 15-year-old a driver's licence just because he can drive a car fast. The adolescent must show that he can drive and navigate traffic safely and that he understands and follows traffic rules. A driving licence is only issued when a person reaches the age of eighteen in Ghana, and with it, he can now legally drive a car. He had the ability, if not the power, to drive a car previously, but now he has the licence to do so in an official, legal, and acknowledged manner.

In the same way, as firearms do not belong in the hands of untrained children, the emergence of sexual ability throughout adolescence does not imply that teens are free to engage in sexual activity whenever they want with whom they want. It's the same as having a driver's licence: there's a sex driver's licence after demonstrating that a person can handle sexuality in a controlled and responsible manner—rather than wild, out of bounds, and with merely selfish purposes - society, including one's parents, grants this licence. Marriage is the name of the driver's licence. Without this licence, sexuality transgresses God's creational order and bounds. It's like trampling on the flowers before they bloom and paying a terrible price for it.

God has an assignment for you. We need to know for certain that God has an assignment for each and every one of us.

"For I know the plans I have for you,"

says the Lord.

His Kingdom assignments are divided into two categories: obligations He bestows on us as His children and specific assignments to each of us to carry out the plans He has for our life. We must align ourselves with Him to perform these responsibilities. To align anything implies making sure it is placed in a straight line. "Let's all be on the same page," we say in the corporate world, which means coming to an accord and cooperating as one. Alignment also refers to putting things in order so that they can work. You won't be able to function or perform if you're misaligned. We must align ourselves with God's heart and His Kingdom purposes to reach our full potential. Even if you are going straight on a straight road, if your car's wheels and steering mechanisms are not aligned, your car will drift as soon as you release the steering wheel.

If you keep driving a misaligned car, your tires will wear out very quickly. The car will also consume more petrol because it is not functioning at its optimum. Similarly, flying an aeroplane with misaligned systems is far riskier than driving a car with mismatched mechanisms. For us to work successfully and efficiently, we need to be aligned. When we come into Kingdom alignment, great things can begin to happen in our lives, but we have to accept the challenge until then. *Jesus says,*

"Whoever wants to be my disciple must deny
themselves and take up their cross daily and
follow me."
Luke 9:23

Alignment speaks of arranging and positioning according to a standard. It alludes to our life being subjected to the King's authority. **Not everyone who encounters Jesus and experiences His power decides to believe Him and follow Him, as we witness in the Gospels**. Alignment is more than a one-time decision; it is a process of life transformation. We have the opportunity to continue to calibrate our lives to God's Word and ways while we travel. The Father desires for us to become like Jesus. **Our motivation comes from our love for Jesus, our respect for Him, and our heart's response to His grace, not from religious performance. Alignment also refers to our place in relation to Father's plan for our lives.**

The Proceeding Patterns

"Do not be conformed to this world, but be transformed by the renewing of your mind, that you may prove what is that good and acceptable and perfect will of God is."
Romans 12:2

HAVE YOU ever felt physically, emotionally, or spiritually out of sorts? Our lives, bodies, hearts, and thoughts can all become out of sync with God's best purposes for us in various ways. When we leave His love, rest, serenity, or even His presence, our lives can rapidly get out of whack on a variety of levels. **Your life is out of balance if you are not progressing.** Many of us are rigorously unaware that our lives are out of balance. We are eager to blame forces outside of ourselves for what isn't working in our lives—circumstances, people, government, and, all too frequently, the enemy. But we allow our lives to become misaligned more often because of socialization, civilizations, and compromise. We defer to our relational pattern, the people we hang around, and how we were raised to determine how high we can advance in life. **You must first alter yourself if you wish to change the flock with which you move. When you change, everything and everyone around you must adjust to fit your growth and progress, and this is a principle. Don't wait for people or circumstances to line with your desires; align yourself first,** and they will follow. Ralph Waldo once said, "Do not go where the path may lead; go instead where there is no path and leave a trail."

Are things the way they are because of who you are? What is that one thing that you can change that can change everything? Could it be that you are the way you are since you have not changed the way you think and the expectations of your old self? How would God's knowledge to use you to impact many people change your thinking about what's possible? **God wants to increase your influence wherever He has positioned you; the only thing is that getting a new cup for the new wine is all you need.** God is actively presenting you with opportunities to expand your control and influence. I motivate you to take advantage of these possibilities because *like Jacob lay hands on his grandson Ephraim in Genesis 48:16,*

> *"as your influence grows, so does your dominion and territory."*

Jacob was not just laying hands on him to prophesy over him and anoint him but also bring his thinking into line. **It's not just about what God will accomplish for you when hands are placed on you; it's also about what God connects you to.** When God places his hands on someone, he is inviting them to help with a mantle correction. A realignment is required to adjust your spiritual cloak. In other words, there is a perception adjustment or "mind alignment" going on—a mental adjustment is required. **Though your mind is spiritual, your brain is physical, and these are in contention with each other, as Apostle Paul said. The only thing is that your**

brain must realign with your spiritual mind. Your brain will battle you every step of the way if God delivers you a word that challenges you to grow. This is why changing a habit is so difficult and difficult! You can't merely quit doing something to break a habit; you have to start doing something new. This is based on the laws of displacement and replacement. The physical brain must be displaced and replaced by a spiritual brain to align with the mind in this circumstance. Meaning, as you are **displacing something, you must replace it with good.** You leave behind a bad habit by replacing it with a good habit.

About God bringing alignment to you so you can grow and increase in your ministry or your scope of influence, it means you will have to change the way you think—you will have to change your carnal mindset to a spiritual mindset to align with the spiritual giftings, potentials, influence and visions, wisdom, and word of knowledge by the Spirit of God. And as you transform your old self to match with God, the culture will have to change—procedures and precedents will have to be modified—but your brain will always want to do things the same way. That is why the most imperative functioning of changing starts with the brain. **Do the same, get the same. Do different, get different.** Once you start changing, your brain will resist. Your neurobiology is the biggest stronghold you will be required to overcome. *The Bible describe it as*

"The desires of the flesh."

So, after you've connected yourself with God, you won't have to worry about the enemy working against you when

God begins to invite you into a world of growth. Too many of us blame the enemy for our inability to change.

Don't you realise that God has given you authority over all of the enemy's schemes and deceptions? Even so, it's unlikely that the devil is pursuing you. More often, it's our wiring; we misfire because we have mis-wired ourselves! **God wants to rewire your mind to enable you to maximize your potential.**

Starting with Mentality

B ACK TO THE STORY of Jacob, when he lays hands on Ephraim and Manasseh, it allows God to reset their thought processes. *Jacob commands a blessing and prophesies:*

> *"God, before whom my father's Abraham and Isaac walked, The God who has fed me all my life long to this day, The Angel who has redeemed me from all evil, Bless the lads; Let my name be named upon them, And the name of my father's Abraham and Isaac; And let them grow into a multitude in the midst of the earth."*
> Genesis 48:15-16

I decree and pronounce that your children will be redeemed from all evil, as will your great-grandchildren and grandchildren, as well as all of your loved ones, not by your hand, but by the Angel of the Lord. Jacob was not only passing on a blessing, but he was also passing on power. Abraham's name and the anointing that had made him powerful and wealthy were being passed down. "How God revolutionised my life, I'm passing it on to you," Jacob was saying. You're going to think in a new way. You're going to think like a powerful, wealthy, influential person." **Your thoughts are a precursor to your lifestyle.** I decree that, however, God shows you that you're going to live in the next decades—I decree and declare that whatever vision He has given you—whatever prophetic word He has spoken over you—you are developing the essential mentality right now! If you desire to be the best in your ministry, you must think like you are the best, you must act like you are the best, influence like you are the best, rule like you are the best. Many of us are terrified of what others would think if we leave the realm God has delivered us from. **Give folks something to talk about, I say!** It all starts with a mindset. Your internal reality will manifest as the reality you encounter on the outside. Whatever your life's circumstances are, don't strive to change them; change your ideas.

"For as he thinks in his heart, so is he"
Proverbs 23:7

Show me your life, and I will show you your thoughts… Are you prepared to align your thoughts with God's divine purpose for your life? Then you got to start to think and act like a king and a priest.

12
FACING THE FUTURE WITH CONFIDENCE

The Confidence Conundrum

SELF-CONFIDENCE understands that you trust your judgment and abilities and that you value yourself and feel worthy, regardless of any imperfections or of what others may believe about you. This inspires us to believe that if we gain knowledge and work hard in a particular area, we will succeed in the future. This type of confidence leads people to accept difficult challenges and keep going in the face of setbacks. But how are you supposed to be confident when you have nothing to feel confident about in life? How can you become confident when you don't have anything to be confident about? For example, how can you feel confident in your new job if you've never done anything like it before? How can you be confident in your social standing if no one has ever liked you before? How can you be confident in your relationship if you've never been in a healthy one before?

On the contrary, confidence appears to be an area where the rich get richer, and the poor stay the fucking losers; they are in life fulfilment. After all, if you have never experienced much social acceptance and lack confidence around new people and society, that lack of confidence will make people think you are close-fitting and weird and not accept you. And seriously, how are you supposed to be confident in your work experience when previous experience is required even to be considered for a job in the first place? The question we ought to ponder about is, if you have always lost in life, then how could you ever expect to win? And if you never expect to win, you will act like a loser. This gives us a clear idea of how our life continues in the order of "THE CONFIDENCE CONUNDRUM". This is the confidence problem, where in order to be purposeful, fulfilled, happy, successful, or loved; firstly, you need to be confident… but to be confident; you need to be purposeful, fulfilled, happy or loved or successful. So, it seems like if you are stuck in one of two loops: either you are already in a loop of happiness and confidence, like this.

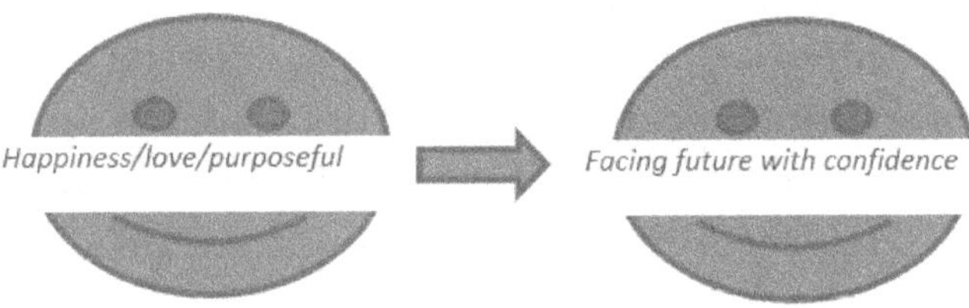

Or you are in a loser loop like this.

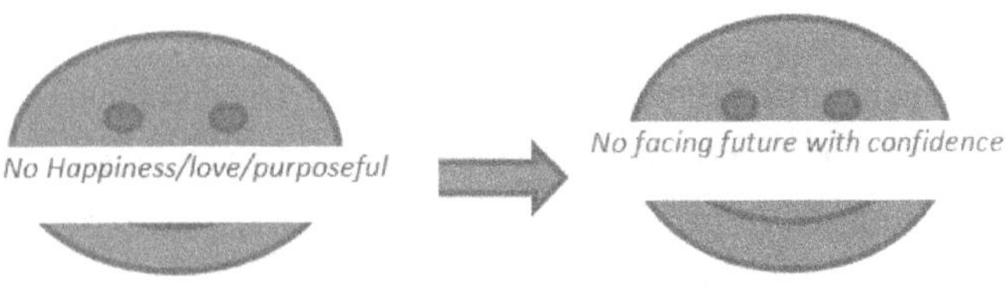

And if you are in the lower loop, well, it seems it is impossible to get out of it.

It's as insane as a dog chasing its tail or trying to cast out your own shadow from you. How possible is this? You can spend time cuticle-gazing trying to sort everything out mentally, but just like with your lack of confidence, you are likely to end up right back where you started. But maybe we are going about this all wrong in the first place. Maybe the confidence conundrum is not a conundrum at all. The obvious and most common solution to the confidence dilemma is to assume that you have all you need. That you already have, or at the very least deserve, what you think you'd need to feel confident.

But this sort of thinking—believing you are already beautiful even though you are a plain good-for-nothing, or believing you are a splendid success even though your only profitable venture was weed distribution in high school—leads to a mindset many people soon realize this does not work. So they take a different approach to face the future. They read articles titled 'the top 50 things confident people do,' then try to do those things. They start to exercise, make more eye contact, dress better, make more and firmer handshakes. This is undoubtedly a step above simply believing that you are already confident and don't belong in the loser loop. After all, at the very least, you're expressing your lack of confidence. And it will work—but only for a limited time as they progress through life.

Again, such reasoning is limited to external sources of assurance. Remember that gaining self-assurance from the outside world is fleeting at best and entirely delusory at worst. So, the remedy to your confidence problem is to stop acting as if you lack nothing and convince yourself that you already have everything you could ever want in life.

I have discovered in life that the only way to be truly confident is to become comfortable with what you lack simply. People who are confident in business are comfortable with failure (failure will not take them by surprise). They understand that failing is a necessary part of learning how their market operates. It is a reflection of their lack of information, not of who they are as individuals. People who are self-assured in their social life are self-assured because they are used to rejection. They are never in any circumstances afraid of rejection because they are comfortable with people not liking them as long as they are expressing themselves honestly and diligently in their spheres of influence. People who are confident in their relationships because they are comfortable with getting hurt, disappointed, rejected, betrayed and abused.

Building Confidence Through Failure

I T IS EASY to lose confidence on the path toward your desired life. In fact, without the right perspective and approach, you will never make it where you want it to go in the future. Something will happen along the way—you will fail, something will not work out as expected or planned, you will hit a glass ceiling. Something will happen, and you will be left with two choices: **Give up or Keep going.** Most people's confidence and faith are shattered by "failures" or "situations," and they surrender their future to a "lesser" but "clearer" path. Rather than completing the task, you might forfeit it (with help)—their confidence and identity shrink. Robert Brault has an amazing quote here: *"We are kept from our goal not by obstacles but by a clear path to a lesser goal."* The hard truth is that then your confidence shrinks, your future shrinks as well. The truth is that the path to happiness also passes through the valley of despair. Those of us who are most at ease with unfavourable experiences are the ones who profit the most in our future selves. We are often concerned that if we get at ease with our failures—that is, if we accept failure as an unavoidable part of life—we will become failures throughout our lives. Does it, however, function that way? We can act without fear, engage without judgement, and love unconditionally if we are comfortable with our failures. The dog lets go of his tail, understanding that it is now a part of him. For ourselves, our families, and society, we all have dreams, goals, aspirations, and longings (as well as worries). But what is it that the future holds in store for you?

Be Confident About Your Future

---

1. Tap into the Confidence you were Born with.

You didn't emerge from the womb unsure of your cry or self-conscious about your protruding umbilical cord. You emerged blissfully ignorant of outside criticism, focused solely on your own experience and desires. You began to have doubts and fears about how other people saw you after you got a sense of self-awareness. You learnt to seek praise and avoid criticism, and if you received more of the latter than the former, you might have become depressed. Remember when you start to doubt yourself: we were all born with confidence, and we can all regain it if we learn to silence the thoughts that threaten it.

2. Trust your Capabilities.

All of us is good at some things and weak at other things. This tells us that no one knows everything. Do not weigh your security against what you know or can do; weigh it against your willingness and capacity to learn more if someone performs better than you; consider it an opportunity to learn from them and even improve yourself. If someone criticizes you, consider it an opportunity to improve. If you fall short on something, understand that you can get closer next time. Do not worry if you are not confident in what you can do now—be confident in your potential and what God has to install for you in the future.

3. Know your Strength and Weakness.

It takes time to figure yourself out. For starters, determining which aspects of yourself are you and who you believe you should be can be difficult. Finding out your talents and weaknesses, as well as what you enjoy doing, is a wonderful place to begin. If you are great in sales, but you actually can't stand sales jobs, then it doesn't matter if you have confidence there. Unless it's all about ego—but does that make you happy? It might help list five things you do well that you enjoy and five things you would like to do well. Work to utilize some of the first lists and work on some of the second each day. You will develop confidence and fulfilment in life as you use your strengths and improve where there's room.

4. Learn to Receive Admiration.

It's astonishing how easy it is to believe all the negative things people around us say and discredit the positive. Taking a compliment is an art. Sometimes, it's instinctive to assume they are just being nice or that maybe you are not skilled— you just got lucky by default. Often, this may be true, but you earn the praise you receive for the most part. Do not persuade yourself not to believe it. Instead, turn it into self-assurance. You performed an excellent job on your work project so that you can do it again. You gave an outstanding performance, indicating that you are gifted and that more is expected of you.

5. Practice Confidence.

Can confidence be put into practice, and with that practice, can you will get better? Your confidence will grow with practice, just like anything else in life. When you meet new people in life, this is a fantastic opportunity to do so. They have no notion who you are, just like if you were a new student at school, so you have an opportunity to show them who you are. Watch your mental monologue as you shake their hand, introduce yourself, and listen to them talk. Replace your doubting thoughts with more confident ones if you find yourself doubting yourself. It's as simple as asking yourself what a confident person would do and then trying to imitate that behaviour. People are more likely to see you the way you want to be seen if they believe you do. You might be confident in some areas but not in others; that's how most of us operate. Draw on your strengths in areas where you are self-assured and adept. Above all, remember that you are capable and worthy—just like everyone else, regardless of what you have accomplished or what mistakes you have made—knowing this logically is the first step toward believing it in your heart. The key to living it is to believe it. And living it is the key to fulfilling your life's potential.

6. Expect Success.

Confidence comes from success—but confidence also combines another quality because you can be successful yet lack confidence in the sense. It requires a mental attitude generate an expectation of success in the future and life fulfilment. And this alone has the capacity to bring about more success, reinforcing the confidence in its cost. Expect success may seem unusual given that you can't foretell the future, but don't we do the opposite all the time? Have you ever gone into a difficult scenario expecting the worst—that something would go wrong, just to be proven wrong? It is imperative to expect the worst because you will not be disappointed if you fail and pleasantly surprised if you succeed. The cue is to find the successes every day, and you'll notice that they increase over time.

The Deliberate Practice

Y OU WON'T become an Olympian by going to the gym every day and completing the same "routine" workout. This is why "habits" aren't always a good thing in and of themselves. You are heading in a "deliberate" and "selected" direction when you use the term "Deliberate Practice." You can't choose and go through a "process" to become someone if you don't have a strong vision of your future. To say that one should "ignore goals" and focus solely on "the process" is, well, poor advice.

This is illogical, lousy advice, and unrepresentative of the future. You can't choose a meaningful procedure if you don't have a goal in mind. Without a goal, it's impossible to engage in or form significant habits. The process is determined by the goal. If done consciously, the "process" is simply you acting as your intended future self. It's about you growing better at being who you want to be—and failing along the way. It's supposed to be difficult to engage in "deliberate practise." It's difficult since chasing a future self requires acting differently from your current and prior selves. You're working hard to grow and become the person you want to be. That is not an easy task. It's also why you require a motivating and helpful workplace. Because you will face walls along the way, you will need supporters to assist you in breaking through your glass ceilings. Many walls, but as you make little progress toward your future self, you will build CONFIDENCE. With each step of confidence, you will believe more and more that you can become who you intend to be.

Moreover, with each step forward, you will also experience an increase in motivation—which is the desire for what you want. In other words, you will want more and more to become the person you plan to be. You'll train your identity and perception over time so that you'll not only perceive the world through the vision of your new identity but also be that person. Anyone who advises you to "ignore goals" is lying. They have goals of their own, and the "process" they're going through is them attempting to become their future selves. "Focus on habits and neglect goals" is an oversimplification. How could you adopt habits purposely and "deliberately" if you neglected your goals? Why begin a writing habit solely for the purpose of writing? Simply admit that you want to be a writer, and that's why you're currently going through the "process" of doing so, one day at a time. Nothing Is Ever Done: Just "Practice" And "Let It Go."

It takes bravery to gain confidence and become the person you want to be. Attempting and trying to blunder forward demands courage. But that's how you gain self-assurance. One thing to remember is that "deliberate practise" means exactly that: PRACTICE. It's fine to make mistakes when you're "practising." It's fine to make mistakes. It's fine if you make a mistake. Another example of bad advice can be found here. People frequently advise you to "let go of" or "ignore" certain consequences. Your goal is to become a better version of yourself in the future. You must become extremely COMMITTED to who you want to be, rather than "ignoring" outcomes. Commitment to your future and your objectives is necessary for success.

Commitment is important to undergo the challenging process of "deliberate practice." "If you are interested, you come up with stories, excuses, reasons, and circumstances about why you cannot or why you will not get there. If you are committed, those go out the window. You just do whatever it takes." Here's how to tell the difference: You must be COMPLETELY DEVOTED to the end outcome. However, you must "let go" of the outcomes you obtain along the route. This isn't to mean you should disregard your findings along the road. No! The outcomes you acquire along the road will show you where you need to change and adjust your "method"! If you are not making progress, then you need to adjust the process. Whatever you are trying to accomplish—you need to throw out imperfect work. You cannot attach to the outcomes along the way, but you must learn from them.

Let it pass when things do not go well!

This is all just "practice!"

You have got this!

Keep going!

Higher!

Notes

Credits

Cover page image:

https://www.istockphoto.com/photo/man-opening-up-his-shirt-gm136519621-7055278

https://www.freepik.com/free-vector/royal-golden-crown-banners-set_16027880. htm#page=1&query=crown&position=5